The Yachtsman's Pilot
North and East Scotland

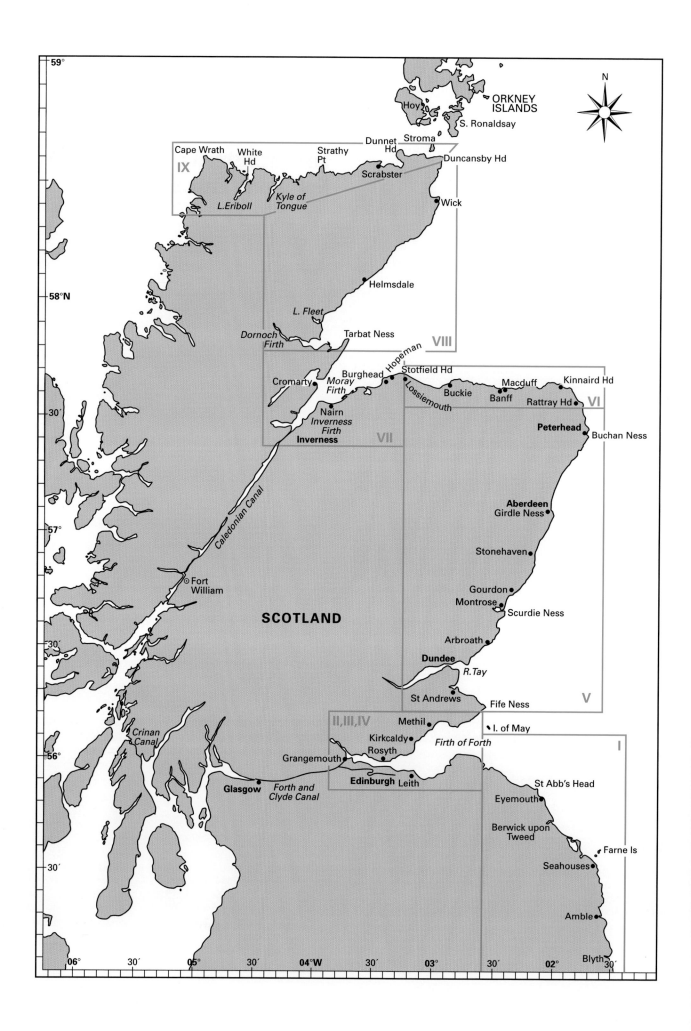

The Yachtsman's Pilot North and East Scotland

The Farne Islands to Cape Wrath

MARTIN LAWRENCE

Imray Laurie Norie & Wilson

Published by
Imray Laurie Norie & Wilson Ltd
Wych House The Broadway St Ives
Cambridgeshire PE27 5BT England
☎ +44 (0)1480 462114 *Fax* +44 (0) 1480 496109
Email ilnw@imray.com
www.imray.com
2003

Martin Lawrence has asserted his right to be identified as the author of this work in accordance with the Copyright, Designs and Patents Act 1988.

The plans and tidal information have been reproduced with the permission of the Hydrographic Office of the United Kingdom (Licence No. HO151/951101/01) and the controller of Her Britannic Majesty's Stationery Office.

ISBN 0 85288 606 3

British Library Cataloguing in Publication Data.
A catalogue record for this title is available from the British Library.

CAUTION
Whilst every care has been taken to ensure accuracy, neither the Publishers nor the Author will hold themselves responsible for errors, omissions or alterations in this publication. They will at all times be grateful to receive information which tends to the improvement of the work.

CORRECTIONAL SUPPLEMENTS
This pilot book will be amended at intervals by the issue of correctional supplements. These are published on the internet at our web site www.imray.com and may be downloaded free of charge. Printed copies are also available on request from the publishers at the above address.

PLANS
The plans in this guide are not to be used for navigation. They are designed to support the text and should at all times be used with navigational charts.

The last input of technical information was January 2003.

Printed in Italy by Eurolitho, SpA, Milan

Contents

Preface

This Pilot follows the series of four volumes by the same author which already cover the west coast of Scotland. It is intended to provide information for boat owners wishing to explore away from the main sea-routes and includes harbours which are only accessible at certain stated of tide and quiet weather, and only to those boats which can take the ground as the tide recedes. There are plenty of harbours, and a few natural anchorages along this coast, although not many in which a boat requiring 2m of water can expect to stay afloat at all states of the tide.

Many of these harbours are not well known to yachtsmen, and not all are comprehensively documented. As well as visits by sea and land, and aerial photography, and consulting harbourmasters and local boat owners, I have consulted unpublished Admiralty surveys and engineers' plans – both sometimes dating from the mid-19th century. In some cases the information is offered as an aid to exploration rather than an aid to navigation and the outcome of subsequent discoveries will be welcome.

This volume covers parts of the coast also described in the *Sailing Directions of the Royal Northumberland Yacht Club*, and the *Pilot Handbook of the Forth Yacht Clubs' Association* and in some cases those publications provide more detail.

Further north, Aberdeenshire Council and Moray and Banff Councils publish jointly a *Directory of Harbours* every year, including tide tables for Aberdeen, with plans of council-owned harbours.

Parts of this coast are charted at a scale no larger than 1:200,000, and even on the south side of the Moray Firth, except for some individual harbours, the largest scale charts are at 1:75,000. In certain areas Ordnance Survey *Pathfinder* maps at 1:25,000 provide valuable information.

Imray, Laurie, Norie and Wilson have published charts and sailing directions for this area for more than a century and a half; the fourth edition of their *Pilot to the East Coasts of England and Scotland* was published in 1854, and the first edition probably predated the first Admiralty *Pilot* for these waters. An advertisement in 1890 for Norie's Nautical Warehouse in London offers 'General Charts on Large Scale', including 'East Coast of Scotland from Cape Wrath to Newcastle, in 3 sheets, with Plans and Book of Directions, 10s 0d.'

Meanwhile the fishing industry has wasted away, with continental boats gaining rights of access to Scottish waters and the UK government not exerting itself much on behalf of local fishermen, who have few votes to offer. Some former fishing harbours are being adapted for leisure use, and local authorities are keen to attract yachtsmen, so that visiting yachts may expect a positive welcome on the northeast coast.

I have consulted local yachtsmen, fishermen, harbourmasters and local authority engineers, and help and advice from the following individuals and organisations is particularly acknowledged: Ron Ball, Mike Roper, Ron Stewart, David Richard-Jones, Andrew Bruce, Dick Fresson, Highland Council, Royal Findhorn Yacht Club, George Morris.

In the absence of detailed charting information, photography and particularly aerial photography, provides an additional dimension, but obtaining it is often not straightforward. Apart from good light and the availability of the aircraft, pilot, photographer and reasonable flying conditions, it is desirable to schedule the operation for a low spring tide when rocks and sandbanks may be visible. Low springs on this coast occur early in the morning, and for a flight over the south side of the Moray Firth I had to leave home long before dawn. Fog was a possibility, and indeed rolled in towards the end of the flight, which is why there are no photos of Sandhaven. An email from the pilot the same evening told me that fog had later closed down Inverness airport.

On another occasion a flight from Wick was planned and with a favourable forecast we drove there from central Scotland, ready for an early start. In the morning the weather was murky, although it cleared in the afternoon, so that all aerial photos from Inverness northward were taken around high water.

Martin Lawrence
Mid Calder
January 2003

Introduction

The north and east coast of Scotland, together with the northeast coast of England, are the least-known parts of the British Isles among yachtsmen, if only because of the small resident population. A comparison might be drawn with the coasts of Kent and Sussex: what, after all, have they to offer except the proximity to a large population and the prospect of a quick trip over to France for less expensive drink?

The coasts of northeast England and southeast Scotland are covered more intimately by the Royal Northumberland Yacht Club's *Sailing Directions*, and the Forth Yacht Clubs Association *Pilot Handbook*, and in those areas the coverage of this volume is limited to harbours likely to be used by visiting yachts, although the photos may be found helpful.

Accommodation specifically for yachts is growing, although it reflects the limited demand. Until very recently most harbours existed principally for commercial use, whether fishing or cargo-carrying. Already, however, more yacht harbours with pontoon berths are established on the northeast coast of Scotland than on the northwest.

Yachts will often share harbours with fishermen and working boatmen, many of whom work under difficult conditions. Some see their livelihoods declining, and are not inclined to suffer fools gladly, especially fools who treat their waters as a playground. Most, however, welcome visitors – if only because they are not yet commonplace – and willingly give any help which may be needed.

The Forth and Clyde Canal has recently been restored for through navigation, albeit with headroom limited to 3m, so that sailing yachts would need to take their masts down, and many motor yachts with high superstructure will be unable to use it. This will make the west coast of Scotland more accessible to visitors from the east coast of England and from the continent of Europe. Outline details of the canal are provided in Chapter IV, and progress and developments will be made known through the customary amendment Supplements and future editions.

This book is intended to be used by seaworthy cruising yachts, sail or power, with a draught of less than 2m. On the Northumberland coast several inshore natural havens and drying harbours which can be visited by small open boats, are detailed in the RNYC *Sailing Directions* and Henry Irving's *Forth, Tyne, Dogger, Humber* (Imray). Likewise the Firth of Forth and the Grampian coast are described in the FYCA *Handbook*. In the Moray Firth, and further north, however, those harbours which could be used by small yachts have been included here.

A boat cruising on this coast must, above all, be robust: any size of boat is suitable if well found, and competently handled. Significantly, Nick Thomson, who compiled the original FYCA *Handbook*, used to sail from the Forth in a heavy traditional 18-foot open boat. (Coincidentally a similar boat appears on the cover of RNYC *Sailing Directions*.) The smallest boats have access to more havens, but for these reference is made to specific local Pilots.

Deep-draught boats will be limited as to the harbours which they can use, but will probably be faster and have greater endurance than smaller shoal-draught boats for which more harbours are available. I doubt whether a really lightweight sailing yacht is suitable for any except limited local cruising within the Firth of Forth or Moray Firth. Similarly, a lightweight motor cruiser, particularly one with a single outboard motor, or with unprotected propellers, will be at a disadvantage.

Yachts traditionally built on the east coast of Scotland are represented by the Fifers from Millers of St Monance, on the lines of small inshore fishing boats, and the Spey class motor sailers from Jones of Buckie.

By contrast, a popular design built on the Firth of Forth is the 22-foot E-boat with a lifting keel. For trailed boats there are launching places in most areas which are suitable for such boats.

Chartering is mainly confined to the Caledonian Canal (although suitably-qualified charterers are allowed to take boats out to sea). It is a reflection on the undeveloped nature of the area that there are few, if any, charter boats based at other places on the east coast of Scotland.

History

The north and east of Scotland has been populated for many thousand years, probably more densely and for longer than in the west, and the area is rich in archaeological remains. The earliest identifiable people were known as Picts, a name given to them by the Romans, who extended their dominions northward briefly in the second century AD. The Romans won a critical battle at Mons Graupius, believed to be situated about 15 miles northwest of Aberdeen. They had overextended their lines of communication, however, and gradually withdrew to the Antonine Wall, which coincides with the line of the Forth and Clyde Canal, and after a few decades they withdrew further south to Hadrian's Wall in Northumberland and Cumbria.

The Picts were left alone for several centuries until Irish Celts expanded into Scotland, introducing Christianity in the sixth century, and founding monasteries such as the one at Holy Island (Lindisfarne) in Northumberland. These monasteries were centres of learning and craftsmanship, and easy targets for the Norsemen who arrived in the ninth century. After they settled in they founded what has been described as a Northern Commonwealth which extended from Greenland to France (where they became Normans). Their influence in Scotland waned after the Battle of Largs in 1263, but Scotland's links remained oriented to the European mainland and away from England, with whom it was usually more or less overtly at war. Over several centuries the town of Berwick-upon-Tweed on the border changed hands more than twenty times.

In 1540 King James IV sent a naval expedition to assert himself over the Lords of the Isles in the west, the significance of which, in the context of this book, is that the first known Sailing Directions for the Scottish coast were compiled for that expedition, by Alexander Lindsay.

The religious upheavals of the Reformation were as traumatic in Scotland as in the rest of Europe. England and Scotland were united under the Stuart kings in the seventeenth century, interrupted by the Civil War, during which the forces of the English 'Protector' Cromwell launched fresh attacks on Scotland. The monarchy was restored in 1660, but the last reigning Stuart king, James II of England and VII of Scotland, abdicated and was replaced by a Dutchman in 1689.

In turn the crown was inherited by the Elector of Hanover, and in 1707 the governments of the two countries were united in a single parliament in London. Now, after three centuries, a devolved parliament sits in Edinburgh. Until 1707 Scots merchants and entrepreneurs had been barred from trading with England's colonies in America and their principal trading links had been through the east coast with mainland Europe. The Stuarts didn't give up, though, and twice, in 1715 and 1745, covertly supported by the French, mounted an invasion. The second 'Jacobite Uprising' was savagely suppressed and followed by further acts of inhumanity such as the Highland Clearances, in which the native people were 'cleared' from the land to be replaced by more profitable sheep.

At the same time, however, a sort of Scottish renaissance occurred, producing a number of writers, philosophers, scientists, engineers, agriculturists, doctors, military officers and colonial administrators quite out of proportion to the size of the population. Among these were engineers such as Thomas Telford, who designed and supervised the Caledonian Canal as well as roads and bridges, and some harbours throughout the Highlands; and the Stevenson dynasty, who are well known for designing and constructing every lighthouse around the Scottish coast and who also had a hand in the design of most of the harbours.

Tides

Tidal streams in the North Sea flood from north to south, taking a full tidal cycle between Pentland Skerries in the Pentland Firth and Dover.

The change in direction of the tidal stream often does not coincide with high and low water, and may be considerably affected by the past or present wind direction and by barometric pressure.

The spring range varies from 3·7 at Aberdeen to 1·9 at Lowestoft, with substantial local variations.

Almanacs may differ in the standard ports for which they provide tidal data; Macmillans, however, uses Wick as a standard port, but this differs from Dover by only 10 minutes.

The *Directory of North East Council Harbours* contains full tide tables for Aberdeen.

Anchorages and mooring

Some harbours which are otherwise suitable for yachts are not accessible in all weather or at all states of tide. A table at Appendix III compares the accessibility of harbours at different states of tide.

Natural anchorages are few and almost none of them give all-round shelter.

Marinas and yacht harbours, although few in number, are more common than on the northwest coast of Scotland.

Berths may be made available in commercial harbours.

It is more common in northeast Scotland than further south for clubs or groups of boat owners to create their own facilities by leasing a disused harbour or taking over (by agreement with the appropriate authority) the management of a sheltered or partly sheltered area for moorings, instead of depending on a commercial operator. Some harbours are considered by their proprietors to be private, and visitors are not welcome.

Transport and crew changes

Rail connections link the south to Newcastle, Edinburgh, Dundee, Aberdeen and some intermediate towns. A separate line from Edinburgh goes to Inverness, Invergordon, Brora, Wick and Thurso.

Car ferry services run to Newcastle from Amsterdam, Hamburg, Göteborg (Gothenburg), Stavanger and Bergen, and to Rosyth in the Firth of Forth from Zeebrugge.

There are air services to Edinburgh from London, Amsterdam, Copenhagen, Stavanger and Bergen, and to Aberdeen from London, Amsterdam, Stavanger and Bergen.

Most towns have some sort of bus service, although visitors from continental Europe will not find these so well integrated with other transport as at home.

Emergencies

Coastguard Marine Rescue Centres are established at Tynemouth, Fife Ness (Forth), Shetland and Aberdeen.

Lifeboats are stationed as follows, being all-weather lifeboats, except those marked (I) which are inshore lifeboats:
Tynemouth, Blyth, Cullercoats (I), Craster (I, summer only), Amble, North Sunderland, Berwick-upon-Tweed, Eyemouth, Saint Abbs (I), Dunbar, North Berwick (I, summer only), Queensferry (I), Kinghorn (I), Anstruther, Broughty Ferry, Arbroath, Montrose, Aberdeen, Peterhead, Macduff, Buckie, Kessock (I), Invergordon, Wick, Thurso (Scrabster), Longhope, Stromness, Kirkwall (the last three in Orkney).

Supplies and services

As the east coast is more densely populated than the west coast of Scotland provisions are more adequately available. With the decline in the fishing industry marine services such as repairs and fuel are likely to be less widely available than hitherto.

Water is usually available on the quayside but often with no hose. It is worth carrying a 20m hose of the type which is stowed flat on a reel, with a universal connector.

Fuel is often available only by road tanker, but the suppliers may serve a yacht if they are delivering at the same time to a fishing boat. The size of hose may be incompatible with a yacht's filler; it is worth also carrying a fuel jerrycan and a funnel of the straight-sided pattern.

Gas is mainly provided by *Calor Gas*, who will only exchange a full container for an empty one. Alternative suppliers are *MacGas* and *J-Gas*, but they don't deal with the smaller sizes. No supplier in the UK will refill your own gas bottle.

Chandlery in sizes appropriate to yachts is limited to places which otherwise cater for yachts.

Boatyards are equally limited, although a yard specialising in working boats may well be able and willing to carry out repairs, often working to a high standard.

Amenities

As the principal sources of employment for local communities has dried up, some of them have turned to the rich heritage left by former activities to feed the tourist trade. Castles (especially around the Anglo-Scottish border) are often objects of great interest, as are ship museums, local museums, Victorian engineering and cities, especially Edinburgh. There are many opportunities for walking, both on established tracks and in the wild further north.

Eating ashore may not often be a memorable gastronomic experience and least likely where captive market such as major tourist attractions. A search through a directory of eating places in Scotland yielded only 17 places with entries on the east coast apart from Edinburgh, Aberdeen and Inverness.

History The east coast encapsulates the history of Scotland, with many examples on the ground: castles and social developments ranging from the clearances to planned villages and the development of communications and the fishing industry.

Cruise Planning

A direct passage made from Great Yarmouth to Peterhead is about 320M.

Visitors might consider a visit to the northeast of Scotland in combination with the west coast, and details of the Caledonian Canal are included.

A yacht might be left at a marina or laid up ashore in Scotland, or afloat in the Caledonian Canal, although account needs to be taken of British Waterways' Boat Safety Scheme, under which a boat intending to spend some time in a canal system (as opposed to passing through) must undergo a survey of safety-related criteria.

For a discussion of alternative courses to the west coast see chapter IX.

The distance from Fraserburgh to Mallaig by Cape Wrath is 290M; by Caledonian Canal it is 202M. The break-even point on distance is about Gairloch. In calculating which way to go account must be taken of the delays in the canal, and the exposure on the north coast of Scotland.

Delivery passage in stages

For a passage in shorter stages, for example over a series of weekends in preparation for a main cruise in northern waters, details of appropriate harbours at which to leave a yacht between stages, and public transport by which to return home, are given in each section.

North of Hartlepool there are now marinas at Sunderland, Tynemouth and at Warkworth (Amble), the last two of which are convenient for trains to the south. The next places at which a yacht might be left for a period are Granton and Port Edgar on the Firth of Forth, but these are some 30 and 40M off a direct passage across the mouth of the firth and arrangements should be made in advance.

Peterhead has a marina; Stonehaven, Aberdeen, and Fraserburgh might be considered in an emergency, the first two having good trains to the south. Yachts have been left for long or short periods at some of the Moray Firth harbours, but communications there are more extended. Inverness has secure marinas, and communications are good, and yachts can be left at Wick or Scrabster if necessary.

Notes on plans and sailing directions

This Pilot includes information about places which can be visited only under favourable conditions. Some are suitable only for shoal-draught boats, such as Drascombe luggers and Cornish crabbers.

It is the skipper's responsibility to decide whether conditions prevailing are in fact suitable for a particular visit.

Charts The range and quality of Admiralty Charts is excellent, although in one or two areas the scale is a bit inadequate for exploring inshore, and their cost puts a severe strain on the cruising budget. This pilot is not intended as a substitute for Admiralty charts. Although many of the plans include more detail than the charts, they only cover small areas, and it is essential to have adequate charts on board. A complete list of current charts is given in Appendix II.

The horizontal datum of Admiralty charts covering the area referred to in this volume is in the process of being changed. The greatest difference in most cases is about 100m, which is enough to miss the entrance of a harbour in poor visibility, or to fail to avoid concealed hazards, especially if the navigator is putting undue faith in the precision of electronic position fixing.

The newer charts are clearly marked WGS 84, and production of editions of charts using this datum began to appear in September 2000.

On some GPS receivers the appropriate datum can be selected; that used by default is WGS 84, but the older datum, OSGB 36, may not always be identified on the chart. This is also the datum for Ordnance Survey maps.

If you have a chart with an unidentified datum and a GPS receiver on which the datum cannot be selected, allow at least 100m margin. Take an early opportunity to calibrate your GPS with a known charted object. Within the area covered by this Pilot the shift from the position given by GPS receivers calibrated to WGS 84 to charts set out to OSGB 36 varies between 0·0 and 0·01 minute northward and between 0·06 and 0·08 minute eastward.

Imray, Laurie, Norie and Wilson publish a full range of charts suitable for passage making, with inset plans of harbours.

Some obsolete Admiralty charts show more detail than any current one, sometimes at a larger scale, but the soundings on them are in feet and fathoms; these are referred to where appropriate. They should of course only be used to supplement current charts, not as a substitute for them. Although many people blithely observe that 'rocks don't move', new ones are discovered (sometimes the hard way), buoys are moved, and new features are constructed ashore. The more charts you have (corrected, of course, up to date) the less anxious your pilotage will be.

Photographs, especially air photos, provide greater detail than can be shown on a plan. Ideally those photos would always be taken at low water springs, in perfect weather, with the light from the direction

Aberdour harbour

which shows the features to the best advantage – and would have been taken shortly before publication. Unfortunately, circumstances often don't work out that way, and some of the photos were taken at high water, or in poor light, or some years previously.

Plans are included of harbours for which plans are not widely available elsewhere. Plans of the more frequently used harbours are included as inserts on Imray charts.

Ordnance Survey *Landranger* maps (1:50,000) and in some cases the new series of OS *Explorer* maps (1:25,000) provide useful additional detail for exploring inshore. These maps are particularly useful on the south side of the Moray Firth, where the largest scale Admiralty chart is at 1:75,000 and further north, where most of the coast is charted at 1:200,000. Reference to *Explorer* maps is given throughout the text where appropriate. For more information see Appendix II.

Tidal information Times of change of tidal streams are related where possible to both a local standard port for accuracy and to Dover for an overall view for longer passages – try planning a passage from the Moray Firth to Cape Wrath based on local standard ports! The Imray *Cruising Almanac* and Reed's *Almanac* refer to Wick as a standard port, but it differs from Dover by only 10 minutes, so the corrections for that port can be applied.

Information on heights of tides is related to local standard ports.

Distances at sea and in canals are given in nautical miles and cables (one-tenth of a mile); distances ashore are in statute miles.

Corrections are published from time to time, go to www.imray.com.

Observations from users are always welcome, and should be sent to the Publishers.

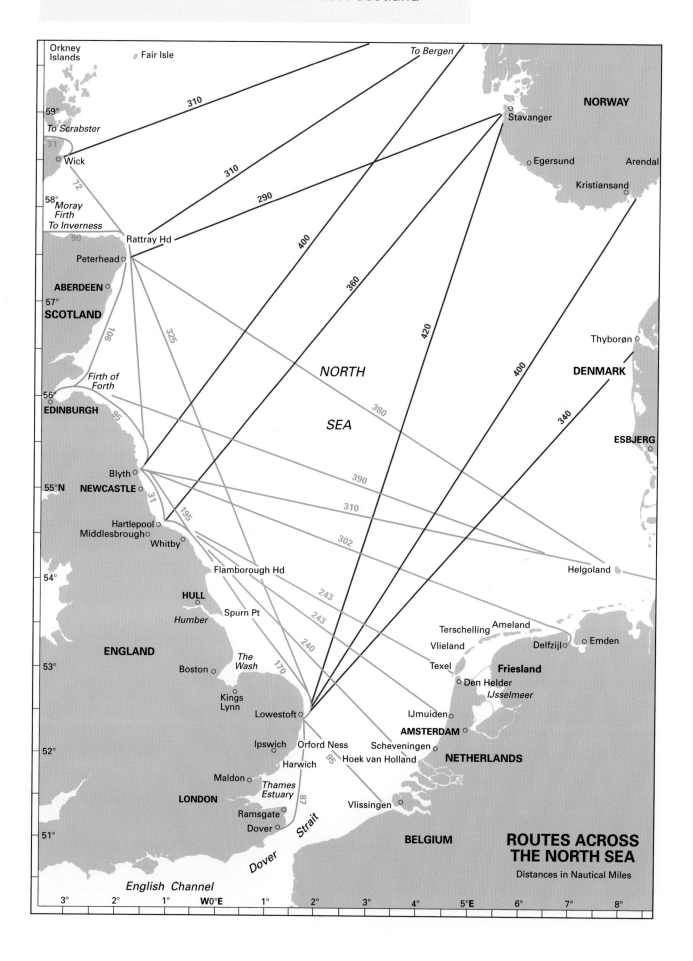

ROUTES ACROSS
THE NORTH SEA

Distances in Nautical Miles

I. Blyth to Bass Rock

Passages from the southern North Sea to Hartlepool

Coming from the south, Hartlepool is the first harbour which gives anything like all-weather access. The marina is in an enclosed basin, reached through a lock, but if this cannot be approached because of weather or tidal conditions, a temporary berth may be found in the North Dock, by arrangement with the harbourmaster.

Hartlepool is also the first harbour on the direct route north at which one might safely leave a yacht, if making a passage in stages.

If you make for Hartlepool, coming from Southeast England or mainland Europe, you have the option of carrying on to Sunderland, Tyne, or Blyth, or diverting to Bridlington, Scarborough or Whitby if circumstances make this desirable. Access to each of the last three is limited by tide and, sometimes, by adverse weather.

Distances to and from Hartlepool are in miles as follows

Great Yarmouth	170
IJmuiden/Den Helder	243
Helgoland	312
Stavanger	360

The next suitable passage harbour is Blyth, 31M from Hartlepool, the headquarters of the Royal Northumberland YC. Alternatives are Sunderland and Tynemouth, as above, or carrying on to Lindisfarne or Eyemouth.

Blyth to Bass Rock

The channel inside Coquet Island is beset by shoals and drying reefs, and a further reef extends N from the island. Most of the buoys here have been withdrawn. For details see below.

The Farne Islands, about 32M north of Blyth, extend over 4M from the coast with an inshore passage navigable in clear weather. The islands are surrounded by off-lying rocks, and the tides run strongly among them.

Longstone Lighthouse, near the E end of the islands, is red with a white band, 26m in height.

Farne Lighthouse, near the SW end of the islands, is a white tower 13m in height.

For the inside passage see below.

Bamburgh Castle, on the mainland west of Farne Lighthouse, is very conspicuous.

Holy Island (Lindisfarne) is low-lying and close inshore. Lindisfarne castle, 6½M WNW of Longstone, is conspicuous, although more modest

St Abb's Head from north

Bass Rock, and the South Carr extending from the shore in the foreground

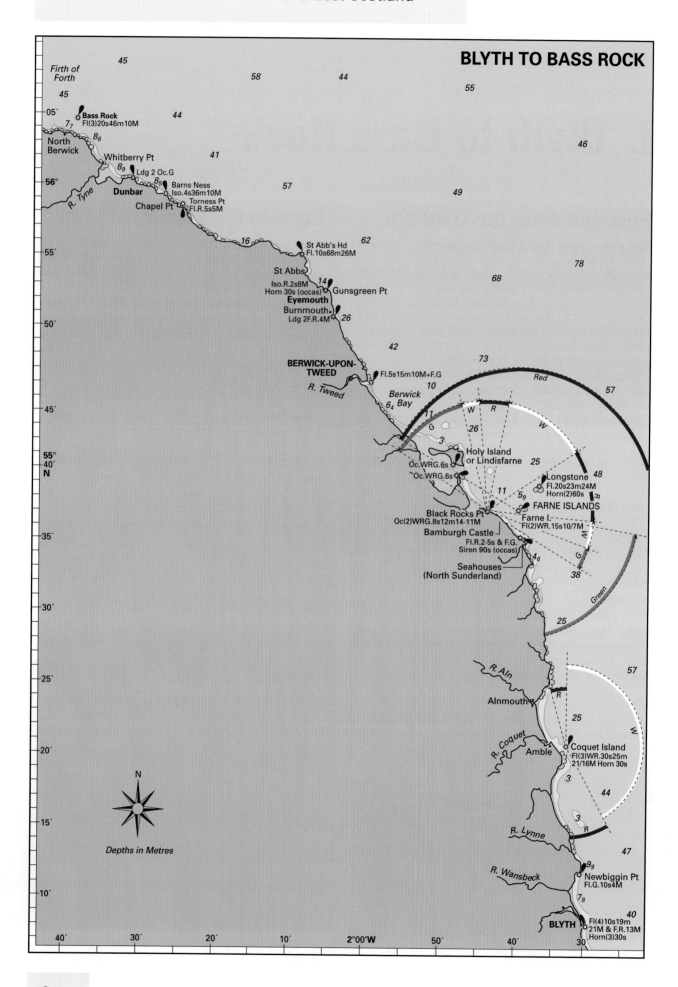

than Bamburgh. Emanuel Head, the NE point of the island, is marked by a beacon with a triangular topmark.

Goldstone, which dries, less than 2M east of Lindisfarne, could be a hazard to a yacht when tacking. It is marked by a buoy on its SSW side (see page 13).

Berwick-upon-Tweed, with towers, spires and a tall chimney to the S of the entrance, lies at the mouth of the River Tweed, 15M NW of Longstone.

St Abb's Head (conspic) with a low white lighthouse at a height of 60m on the hillside, stands 9M N of Berwick.

Torness Nuclear Power Station stands 10M NW of St Abb's Head, with Barns Ness Lighthouse 1½M beyond.

Bass Rock, 115m high, stands a mile offshore at the S side of the entrance to the Firth of Forth, 10M NW of Torness.

Lights on passage

Blyth East pier head Fl(4)10s19m21M+F.R.13m13M Horn(3)30s
Coquet Is Fl(3)WR.30s25m21/16M Horn 30s
Black Rocks, Bamburgh Oc(2)WRG.12m14-11M
Longstone, Farne Is Fl.20s23m24M Horn(2)60s
St Abb's Head Fl.10s68m26M
Barns Ness Iso.4s36m10M
Isle of May Fl(2)15s73m22M

If it should be necessary to break a passage or leave a yacht for a period, Warkworth has a convenient and safe marina, although the harbour entrance is hazardous in onshore winds and outwith 3 hours either side of HW.

For the passage from St Abb's Head to Montrose see Chapter V, page 47.

Apart from commercial, naval and fishing traffic the only hazard on this passage is the Bell Rock, 12M east of the mouth of the Firth of Tay.

For Isle of May see Chapter III.

Other anchorages and boat harbours may be found between Blyth and Warkworth in calm weather with the aid of the RNYC *Sailing Directions* and OS Explorer *325*.

Warkworth (Amble)

⊕ 6 cables NE of Coquet Island lighthouse 55°20'·5N 01°31'·5W

An artificial harbour at the mouth of the river Coquet with a shoal entrance between pier heads, and a marina in which the water is retained by a sill, providing complete shelter from the weather once inside.

Charts

BA *1627* (1:6,250); Imray *C24* (plan); OS Landranger *81*

Tides

The south-going stream begins about –0515 HW Tyne (–0045 Dover)

The north-going stream begins about +0045 HW Tyne (+0515 Dover)
Constant –0020 HW Tyne (+0410 Dover)
Heights in metres

MHWS	MHWN	MTL	MLWN	MLWS
4·0	4·1	3·0	2·0	0·8

Dangers and marks

The passage between Coquet Island and the mainland is obstructed by reefs and the channel ½M wide is no longer buoyed.

North Steel, a drying reef, extends ¼M north of the island. and Steel Bush, a submerged rock, lies 4 cables NNE of the island.

Pan Bush Shoal lies ½M off the harbour entrance, with a least depth of 0·3m, and southwest of the shoal a red can light buoy marks the end of a sewer outfall.

The least depth in the harbour entrance varies, but may be as little as 0·1m. If there is any sea running the entrance should not be attempted more than 3 hours either side of HW.

Approach

From south pass half a mile east and northeast of Coquet Island. Continue on this heading for ¼M before turning SSW for the harbour entrance. A passage south of Pan Bush Shoal by way of the sewer outfall buoy should only be taken in settled conditions and only if the buoy is unambiguously identified.

From north identify and pass east of Boulmer Stile red can buoy, then steer 200° for the harbour entrance.

Lights

Coquet Island LtHo Fl(3)WR.30s21/16M; for sectors see plan
Sewer outfall buoy Fl.Y
North pier head Fl.G.6s12m6M
South pier head Fl.R.5s9m5M

At night

The approach is difficult without precise position-fixing equipment and unless the weather is clear enough for the unlit buoys to be identified, Blyth is more convenient.

Berth outside other vessels at south quay, after enquiring about their intended movements, or at Braid Marina, further up the river on the south side. The water level in the marina is retained by a sill the depth over which is shown by a gauge. Make fast temporarily at the fuel berth immediately inside the marina.

This is a good place to leave a boat if necessary for a few days to break a delivery passage, and Alnmouth station is a short journey by taxi or bus, although few long-distance trains stop there. Local trains to Newcastle and Berwick stop at Alnmouth.

Supplies water petrol and diesel, *Calor Gas* and chandlery, telephone, all at marina; shops PO, hotels in town.

Harbourmaster VHF Ch 14 (0900–1700 Mon–Fri). Office at south quay. Braid Marina VHF Ch 80, 37 (24 hours).

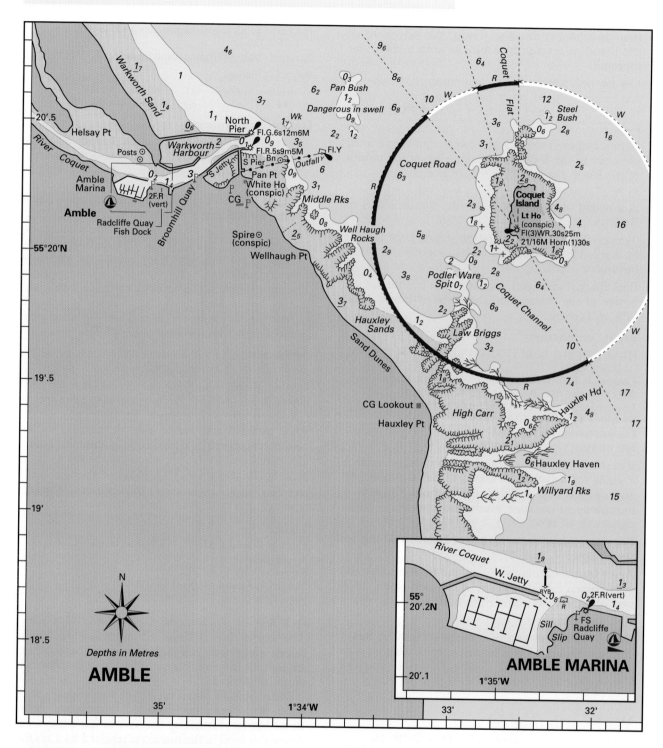

AMBLE

Depths in Metres

AMBLE MARINA

Seahouses (North Sunderland)

⊕ 55°35'·3N 01°38'·8W, ¼M north of the NE breakwater

A drying harbour two miles south of Farne Island, which dries and is only suitable in settled weather for yachts which are able to take the ground.

Charts

BA *111* (1:35,000); Imray *C24* (plan); OS Landranger *75*; OS Explorer *340*

Tides

Constant –0040 HW Tyne (+0338 Dover)
Heights in metres

MHWS	MHWN	MTL	MLWN	MLWS
4·8	3·7	2·7	1·6	0·7

Dangers and marks

Reefs extend 1½ cables NE from the NE breakwater.

Approach

From south keep at least ¼M off the NE breakwater, in a depth of not less than 5m and approach from north, not below half flood. Make fast temporarily in the outer harbour and consult the HM before berthing finally.

Lights
Breakwater Fl.R.2·5s6m
NW pier head F.G.11m3M

Supplies
Water, petrol and diesel, *Calor Gas*, telephone at marina. Shops, PO, in town.
Harbourmaster VHF Ch 14.

Farne Islands
⊕ 1M E of Longstone 55°39'N 01°33'W
⊕ 6 cables south of Farne Is. 55°36'·3N 01°39'W

Owned by the National Trust, and managed by the RSPB as a bird reserve, landing is permitted only at Farne Island, the most southwesterly of the group, and at Longstone, the most northeasterly.

In clear weather the passage between Farne Islands and the mainland may be taken, and the anchorage at the Inner Farne Island is worth a visit, even for a yacht on passage.

Charts
BA *111* (1:35,000); Imray *C24*; OS Landranger *75*

Tides
Run strongly among the Farne Islands and unless taking the Inner Sound they should be passed well to the east.
A mile NE of Longstone spring tides run at 3½–4 knots, and in the Inner Sound they run at 2½ knots.
The SE-going stream begins about −0430 Tynemouth (+0000 Dover).

The NW-going stream begins about +0130 Tynemouth (−0600 Dover).
Constant -0045 Tynemouth (+0345 Dover)

Heights in metres

MHWS	MHWN	MTL	MLWN	MLWS
4·8	3·8	2·7	1·5	0·6

Dangers and marks
Longstone lighthouse, near the northeast end of the group, white with a red band, is conspicuous.

The Knivestone, which dries 3·5m, and Whirl Rocks which are submerged extend ¾M northeast of the lighthouse.

Unless making for the Farne anchorage or Holy Island the more straightforward course is to pass at least a mile east of Longstone.

Inner Sound
⊕ on boundary of white and green sectors of Black Rock bn 55°33'·5N 01°35'W

Red can light buoys north and east of North Sunderland on the mainland, south of Farne Islands, mark reefs extending from the mainland.

Swedman green conical light buoy lies northwest of the Swedman reef, about 1½M northwest of Farne Island.

Bamburgh Castle on the mainland west of the Farne Islands, is conspicuous.

Black Rock light beacon stands about 6 cables NW of Bamburgh Castle.

Farne Islands from east

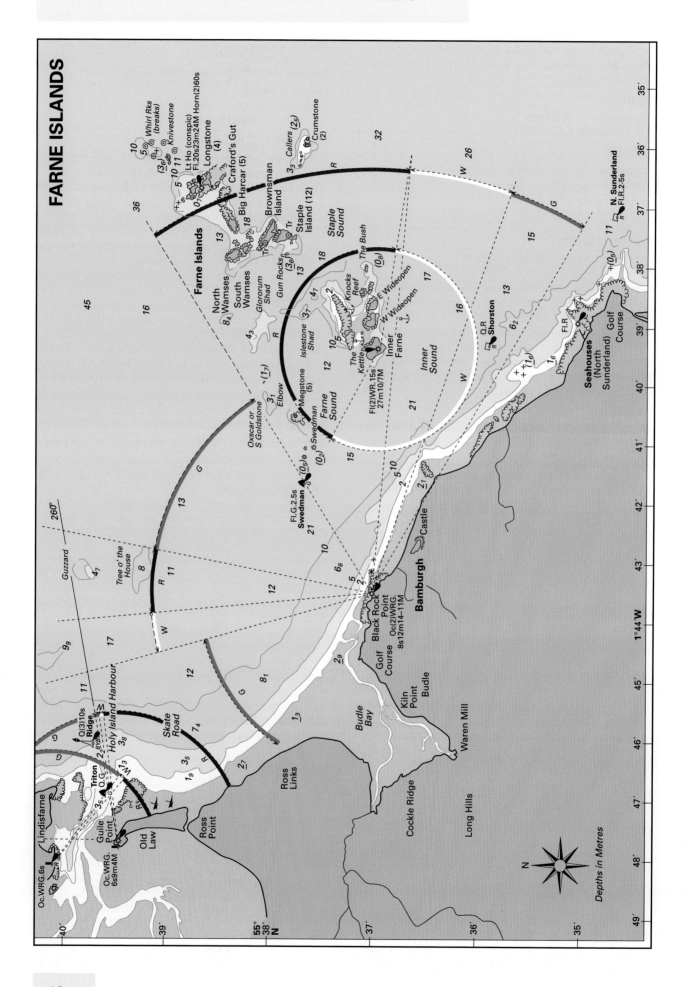

FARNE ISLANDS

Farne Islands

Whirl Rks (breaks)
Knivestone
(3_6) 5 10 11
Longstone (4)
Lt Ho (conspic)
Fl.20s23m24M Horn(2)60s
Craford's Gut
0_7 5
Callers (2_5)
Crumstone (2)
3_3
Big Harcar (5)
18
Brownsman Island
Tr
13
Staple Island (12)
Staple Sound
32
North Wamses 8_4
South Wamses
Glororum Shad
Gun Rocks (3_6) 13
The Bush
(0_8)
26
W
R
36
16
45
4_3
R
Islestone Shad 3_7
4_7 2
Knocks Reef
E Wideopen
W Wideopen
Inner Farne
17
G
15
13
6_2
Megstone (5)
Elbow
3_1
(1_7)
10 5
The Kettle
12
Inner Sound
6_6
16
Q.R
Shorston
Fl.R
(0_5)
Farne Sound
21
Fl(2)WR.15s 27m10/7M
W
N. Sunderland
Fl.R.2.5s
Oxscar or S Goldstone
Swedman (0_2)
15
5 10
$+(0_5)$ 11
Fl.G.2.5s Swedman
21
(0_5)
G
Seahouses (North Sunderland) Golf Course
$+$ 1_6
Fl.R
1_6
$+$
6_6
5 2_1
2_5
13
260°
G
R 11
Tree o' the House
8
Guzzard
4_7
10
12
6
5 2_1
2_9
Black Rock Point
Bamburgh Castle
1_3
G
W
R
17
9_9
11
12
8_1
Skate Road
7_4
Golf Course
Budle
Kiln Point
Waren Mill
Lindisfarne
Oc.WRG.6s
Oc.WRG. 6s9m4M
Triton
Q.G
3_5
2^{By}_3
Q(3)10s
Ridge
Holy Island Harbour
3_8
M
3_5
R
1_9
2_1
Ross Links
Guile Point
Old Law
Ross Point
Budle Bay
Long Hills
Cockle Ridge

Oc.(2)WRG. 8s12m14-11M
Black Rock Point

N

Depths in Metres

55° 38' N

Passage east of Holy Island

Dangers and marks

Goldstone, marked on its SW side by a starboard-hand light buoy.

Plough Seat, a drying reef, 6 cables east of Holy Island, is marked on its east side by a port-hand light buoy.

Goldstone Channel lies between these two buoys.

Plough Rock, which dries 2·6m, west of Plough Seat, is marked by a west cardinal buoy, with a clear passage 3 cables wide west of it.

Approach

If taking the passage inside Farne Islands the two port-hand light buoys north and east of North Sunderland must be identified and left to the southwest and *Swedman* light buoy left to the east.

Pass between the unlit *Goldstone* buoy and the lit *Plough Seat* buoy, 2½M further NNW, or pass at least ½M east of *Goldstone* buoy.

From north identify Emanuel Head at the northeast of Holy Island, on which stands a conspicuous beacon, and then *Plough Seat* light buoy, 1¼M southeast, and pass through the Goldstone Channel.

Pass west of *Swedman* starboard-hand light buoy,

and beware of Islestone reef 3 cables offshore east of Bamburgh Castle, and pass northeast of *North Sunderland* and *Shoreston Outcars* light buoys.

Lights

North Sunderland light buoy Fl.R.2·5s
Shoreston Outcars light buoy Q.R
Longstone LtHo Fl.20s23m24M Horn(2)60s
Inner Farne Fl(2)WR.15s27m10/7M
Swedman light buoy Fl.G.2·5s
Black Rocks Point, on the mainland northwest of Bamburgh Castle, Oc(2)WRG shows white over the fairways, red over Goldstone and Farne Islands, white over clear water between them, and green inshore but is obscured south of 300°.
Ridge light buoy, SE of Holy Island Q(3)10s
Goldstone unlit con buoy
Plough Seat light buoy Q.R.

At night

In clear quiet weather Black Rocks light beacon, together with light buoys, should give enough help to pass through the Inner Sound or to come to the Kettle anchorage.

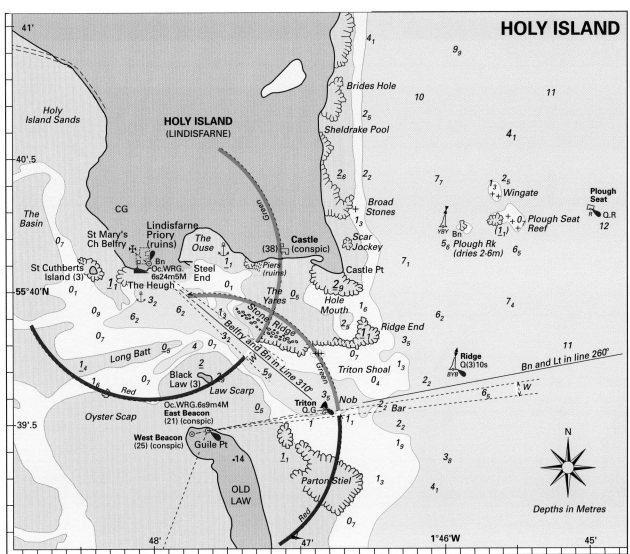

Lindisfarne approach from east

Lindisfarne anchorage from south. Old Law beacons in the foreground

Holy Island

⊕ 55°39'·6N 01°45'·7W close SE of Ridge End buoy

Like the Farne Islands, a unique place, well worth a visit from a passing yacht.

Charts

BA *111* (1:35,000); Imray *C24* (plan); OS Landranger *75*; OS Explorer *340*

Tides

Streams run strongly in the entrance:
the west-going stream begins about +0510 Tynemouth
  (+0445 Dover).
the east-going stream begins about −0045 Tynemouth
  (+0345 Dover).
Constant −0045 Tynemouth (+0345 Dover)

Heights in metres

MHWS	MHWN	MTL	MLWN	MLWS
4·8	3·7	2·7	1·5	0·6

Dangers and marks

(see also Farne Islands above)

Long Ridge, rock, lies on a line extending east to west 3 cables south of the island.

Parton Steel, a drying reef, extends 1½ cables from the northeast side of Old Law, a sandy promontory on the south side of the entrance.

Sandy shoals extend from both sides leaving a narrow channel with a bar on which there is little more than 2m.

Ridge east cardinal light buoy marks the east limit of shoals on the north side of the entrance.

Triton green conical light buoy marks the north side of the channel at the bar.

Two stone obelisks, 25 and 21m high, on Old Law are conspicuous.

Holy Island Castle and the ruined Priory are conspicuous.

Heugh beacon, a framework tower with a red triangular topmark, stands south of the priory ruins on Holy Island.

Approach

See Inner Sound, above.

Old Law beacons kept in line bearing 260° lead over the bar. After passing *Triton* light buoy bring *Heugh* beacon on the south shore of Holy Island into line with the Priory belfry bearing 310°, and steer on that bearing until within a cable of the island.

The anchorage is exposed to SW, especially near HW, and may be uncomfortable, particularly with a SW wind and a flood tide. Subject to weed, and two anchors are needed because of the tide.

Lights

Old Law front beacon Oc.WRG.6s9m4M, 262°-W-264°.

Heugh beacon Oc.WRG.6s24m5M, 308°-W-311°

Supplies

Shop and pubs in village.

Berwick-upon-Tweed

⊕ 55°45'·8N 01°58'·5W ¼M ESE of breakwater head

Charts

BA *175* (1:75,000); *1612* (plan); Imray *C24* (plan); OS Landranger *75*; OS Explorer *346*

Tides

The in-going stream begins about +0515 Tynemouth
  (−0330 Dover).
The out-going stream begins about −0100 Tynemouth
  (−0245 Dover).
Constant −0045 Tynemouth (+0345 Dover)

Heights in metres

MHWS	MHWN	MTL	MLWN	MLWS
4·7	3·8	2·6	1·3	0·6

Dangers and marks

The entrance, on the south side of a stone breakwater at the head of which stands a stone

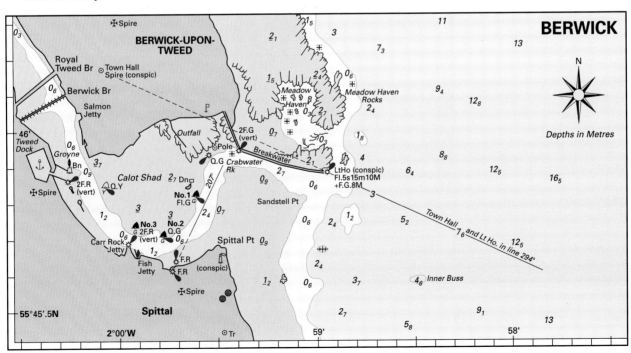

light beacon, is shallow.

Drying rocks extend up to a cable ENE, and 3 cables NNE, of the beacon.

Drying banks extend from Spittal Point at the south side of the entrance to within 50m of the breakwater.

Towards the root of the breakwater the channel runs SSW and gradually bends to northwest; its west and north sides are marked by green conical buoys, some of which are lit.

A conspicuous chimney stands on Spittal Point.

Approach

From any direction keep outwith the 10-metre line until the light beacon on the breakwater head is in line with a spire in the town bearing 293°30'.

At half tide the depth on the bar, which lies SSW of the light beacon, is about 3·4m.

Keep about 15m from the breakwater until the Elbow, where it trends away northward, at which point alter course gradually to port towards the pile beacon at the north end of an islet on the west side of the channel.

Berwick-upon-Tweed from south. Tweed Dock in foreground

Berwick-upon-Tweed. Approach from east

Steer about 207° to pass east of the first green conical buoy, with two beacons to the west of Spittal Point (orange with black bands, with triangular topmarks) in line ahead, then bear to starboard to pass south of the next green conical buoy, but do not take a direct line between them. The beacons may not show the present line of the channel, and the east side of the channel should be marked by unlit red buoys.

Lights

Pier head beacon Fl.5s15m10M F.G.8m1M
Breakwater elbow 2F.G(vert)2m
Channel beacon Q.G.4m1M
G con buoy Fl.G
G con buoy Q.G
Spittal Ldg beacons *Front* F.R.4m *Rear* F.R.9m
Carr Rock jetty 2F.R(vert)
Tweed Dock south pier 2F.R(vert)

Shelter

It is only good in Tweed Dock, the gates of which have been removed, and yachts have to dry out alongside.

Supplies

Water at Tweed Dock, petrol and diesel at garages or by road tanker. Shops, PO, telephone, hotels in town. EC Thursday.

Harbourmaster VHF Ch 12. Office at Tweed Dock.
☎ 01284 307404.

Burnmouth

⊕ on leading line 55°50'·7N 02°03'·5W

A drying harbour at the foot of cliffs about 5M NNW of Berwick.

Ross Carrs, rocks which dry 1·5m, lie 3 cables offshore, north of the leading line.

White beacons on the hillside above in line bearing 253° lead through the entrance channel.

A sharp turn to port leads into the harbour.

At night

The leading beacons show fixed red lights, and the west pier head shows 2F.G(vert).

Eyemouth

⊕ 55°53'N 02°05'·3W 3 cables close W of leading line, 3 cables NW of Buss Craig

Charts

BA *160* (1:75,000), *1612* (1:7,500); Imray *C24* (plan); OS Landranger *67;* OS Explorer *346*

Tides

Constant −0015 Leith (+0330 Dover)

MHWS	MHWN
4·7	3·7

Dangers and marks

Hurcar Rocks, above water and drying, lie up to ¼M north and northeast of the entrance, and reefs extend ¾ cable from the west shore. A north cardinal light buoy lies north of Hurcar Rocks.

The harbour entrance is dredged to 3m.

Burnmouth from west

Approach

Fishing boats may be leaving or entering harbour, and the harbourmaster may not be able to respond to calls on VHF.

From north identify Hurcar north card light buoy, and approach with caution until leading marks (orange triangles, bearing 174°) are identified, and follow this line to the entrance.

From east the deep passage south of Hurcar is not marked, and a course north of those rocks is preferable for a stranger.

The entrance is 15m wide. Inside the breakwaters a submerged training wall on the west side of the channel are marked by pile light beacons, and the channel bends to SSW concealing boats which may be leaving the harbour.

Eyemouth harbour approach, from Hare Head

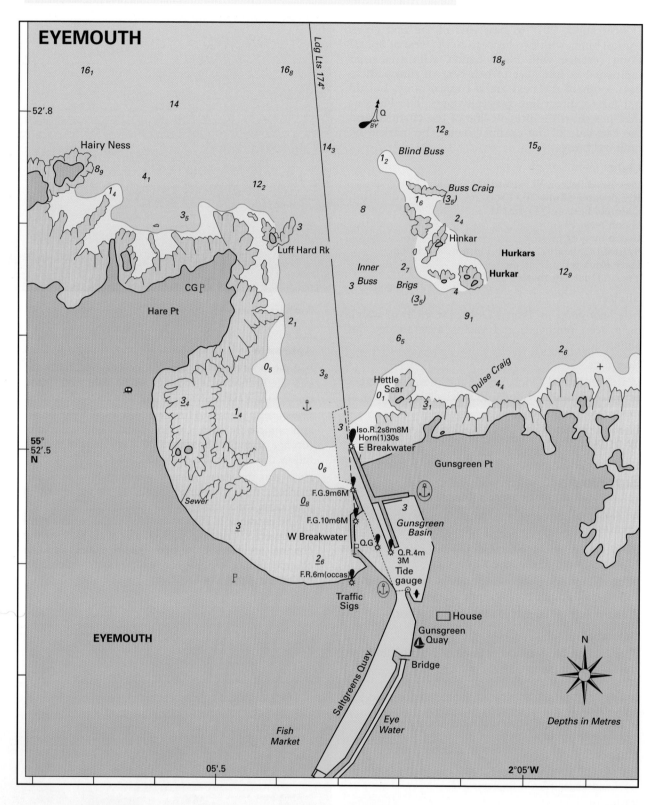

EYEMOUTH

Yachts berth at Gunsgreen Quay on the east side of the harbour. A movable footbridge lies across the mouth of Eye Water, and access may be needed around high water to the boatyard further up the river.

Lights
Hurkar Rocks north card buoy Q
Ldg Lts 174° F.G.9/10m6M (front and rear)
East breakwater head Iso.R.2s8m8M Horn 30s

At night
Identify the N card light buoy off the Hurcars, and then the leading lights, and follow these into the harbour.

Shelter
Excellent, once inside.

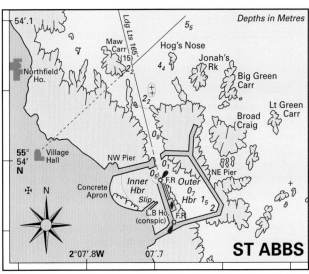

Eyemouth harbour. Yacht berths at Gunsgreen Quay

Supplies

Water at quays, petrol at garages; diesel by road tanker. *Calor Gas* at caravan site (west side of bay), shops, supermarket, telephone, boatyard, engineering services; RNMDSF.

Harbourmaster VHF Ch 12. Office at north end of the west quay. ☎ 01890 750223.

St Abbs

55°54'N 02°08'W

St Abbs lies only 2M north of Eyemouth and is less accessible or convenient, although it may be found more attractive. It has become popular with divers and tends to cater for their needs.

Tides

See Eyemouth

St Abbs harbour approach

Dangers and marks

Drying reefs surround the harbour.
Northfield House, north of the village, is conspic.
Maw Carr is a prominent rock north of the entrance.

Approach

From south head for Bird Cliff, south of St Abb's Head, until Maw Carr is abeam; bring the red-roofed village hall in line with the south side of Maw Carr bearing 228° to clear Hog's Nose rocks to east of the entrance, and keep on or north of that line until the entrance opens up, and steer with the Lifeboat House in line with the head of the NW pier bearing 167°.

From north identify Maw Carr, pass close east of it; and identify the leading marks above.

The entrance is 6m wide.

Lights

Ldg Lts F.R stand at the head of the middle pier and in the SW corner of the Inner Harbour.

Supplies

Water at quay, shop.
Harbourmaster ☎ 01890 771708.

Cove

55°56'N 02°21'W

This is a drying harbour with no facilities, only accessible to shoal-draught boats within two hours of high water. The photo, taken at LWS, shows the features of the harbour.

Dunbar

⊕ on leading line ¼M NNW of rocks 57°00'N 02°30'·8W

An ancient trading and fishing – including whaling – harbour.

The harbour entrance is narrow and part of the harbour dries, but if a secure berth can be found this is a convenient place from which to visit Edinburgh, and for crew changes, as some main-line trains stop there.

A swell comes into the harbour with strong winds between WNW and east. In these conditions boats are moved to the Old Harbour which is better sheltered but dries completely.

Charts

BA *735* (1:25,000); Imray *C23*, *C27*; OS Landranger *67*; OS Explorer map *351*

Tides

Constant –0015 Leith (+0330 Dover)
Heights in metres

MHWS	MHWN	MTL	MLWN	MLWS
4·2	4·2	3·0	2·0	0·7

Dangers and marks

Outer Bush, which dries, lies 3 cables northeast of Dunbar.
A line of rocks, above water and drying, lies up to a cable off the harbour and 2 cables offshore further west.

Cove – very much an occasional harbour

Dunbar harbour from west

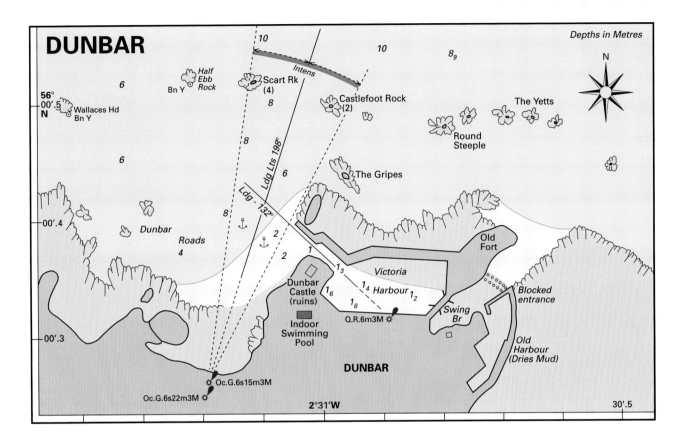

Scart Rock and Castlefoot Rock, north of the harbour entrance, are always above water.

Leading beacons on shore with orange triangle topmarks, points together, bearing 198°, lead between these rocks.

Half Ebb Rock and Wallace's Rock, which cover, to the west are marked by yellow perches.

Approach

From southeast keep at least ¼M off shore until Scart Rock and Castlefoot Rock are identified. Pass between them heading SSW until the harbour opens up and steer southeast into the harbour close to the face of the north pier.

From northwest keep rather further offshore until the beacons on Half Ebb Rock and Wallace's Rock have been identified and pass between them, heading southeast towards the harbour.

Lights

Ldg Lts 198° Oc.G.6s5/22m3M 188°-intens-208° lead between Scart Rock and Castlefoot Rock.

A light on the south side of the harbour Q.R.6m3M shows though the harbour entrance bearing 132°.

At night

These lights in sequence lead into the harbour.

The north side of the harbour dries and on the south side the deepest water is at the west end.

Anchorage may be had in offshore winds south of the line into the harbour.

Supplies

Water; petrol from garage, diesel by tanker, *Calor Gas*, shops, PO, telephone in town. EC Wed. Trains to Edinburgh and south; bus to Edinburgh; air service from Edinburgh. Chandlery at Inner harbour.

Dunbar, on the leading line, looking to seaward

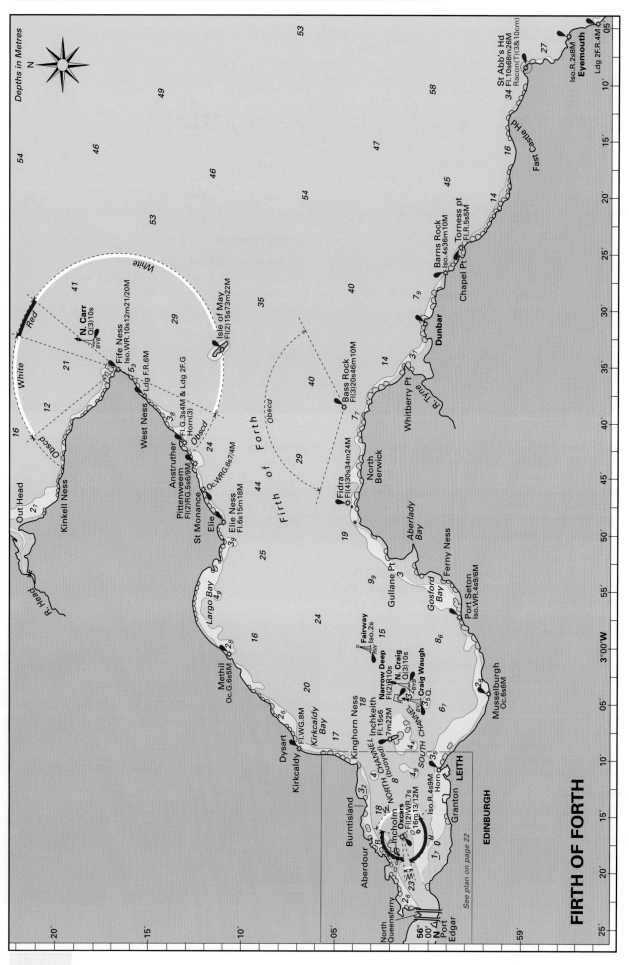

Depths in Metres

N

FIRTH OF FORTH

53

49

54

46

46

53

54

41

White

Red

N. Carr
Q(3)10s
BYB

Fife Ness
Iso.WR.10s12m21/20M

White

Obscd

16

12

21

Out Head

Kinkell Ness

R. Head

5₃

Ldg F.R.6M

Isle of May
Fl(2)15s73m22M

35

29

White

West Ness
3₈

Anstruther
Fl.G.3s4M & Ldg 2F.G
Horn(3)

24

Obscd

Pittenweem
Fl(2)RG.5s6/9M

St Monance
Oc.WRG.6s7/4M

Elie

Elie Ness
Fl.6s15m18M

3₉

Obscd

Firth of Forth

44

29

40

40

Bass Rock
Fl(3)20s46m10M

7₇

Fidra
Fl(4)30s34m24M

14

North Berwick

37

R. Tyne

Whitberry Pt

7₉

Dunbar

58

47

45

Barns Rock
Iso.4s36m10M

Torness pt
Fl.R.5s5M

Chapel Pt

14

16

Fast Castle Hd

27

St Abb's Hd
Fl.10s68m26M
Racon(T)(3&10cm)

34

Iso.R.2s8M
Eyemouth

Ldg 2F.R.4M

05'

27

Largo Bay
4₉

25

19

Aberlady
Bay

9₉

Gullane Pt

3

Gosford
Bay

Ferny Ness

Port Seton
Iso.WR.4s9/6M

16

Methil
Oc.G.6s5M

2₈

24

Fairway
Iso.2s
HW

15

N. Craig
Q(3)10s

Narrow Deep
Fl(2)R10s
BYB

13

3₅ Q.

Craig Waugh
BYB

8₆

6₇

2₇

Musselburgh
Oc.6s6M

Dysart

Kirkcaldy
Fl.WG.8M

2₅

Kirkcaldy
Bay

17

8

20

Kinghorn Ness

18

Inchkeith
Fl.15s6
7m22M

NORTH CHANNEL
(buoyed)

4₁

4₄

4₉

3₅

Horn

SOUTH CHANNEL

6₇

LEITH

Iso.R.4s9M

EDINBURGH

Granton

Aberdour

Burntisland

3₂

18

W

Inchcolm
Fl(2)WR.7s

Oxcars
Q.16m13/12M

1₇

0

See plan on page 22

North
Queensferry

N.
00'

Port
Edgar

2₆

23

59'

56°

20'

15'

10'

05'

3°00'W

55'

50'

45'

40'

35'

30'

25'

20'

15'

10'

05'

II.   Firth of Forth: south

The Firth of Forth is a complete cruising area in itself, with several attractive towns and villages on its shores, although mostly on the north shore.

To make the best of cruising in the Forth takes a not too delicate shallow draught boat able to take the ground.

Even on passage at least a visit to Isle of May and Anstruther might be considered; Edinburgh can be reached easily by public transport from Dunbar.

For regular users or a more extended cruise the Forth Yacht Club's Association *Pilot Handbook* (see Appendix) is essential, although the photos here will supplement that publication.

Charts

Imray chart *C27* covers the Firth of Forth west of a line between Barns Ness and North Carr very adequately for a visitor, with inset plans of the harbours in Chapters II and III.

Admiralty chart *735* covers the outer firth as far as Oxcars, including the approaches to Granton and Burntisland at 1:25,000; OS Explorer map *351*.

Landmarks

Bass Rock, a conspicuous islet 115m high, lies a mile from the shore at the south entrance to the firth.

Isle of May, a mile in length, lies 4M from the shore at the north side of the entrance to the firth.

North Berwick Law, a conical hill, 185m high, might in misty weather, be mistaken for the Bass Rock.

Inchkeith, an island 6 cables long lies 16M west of the Bass Rock in the middle of the firth.

Cockenzie Power Station, with two chimneys 152m high, stands on the shore S of Inchkeith.

Shelter

Is limited, but if adverse weather is anticipated, complete shelter may be possible in the enclosed docks at Methil and Burntisland – all depending on tidal restrictions and the consent of the harbourmaster. Shelter subject to some surge is available at Port Edgar (see Chapter IV) and the harbour is accessible at all states of the tide. Shelter is available in the harbour at Anstruther, which has pontoons, although it dries.

Granton is accessible at all states of tide but much of the harbour dries. A pontoon is provided for visiting yachts on the east side of Middle Pier.

There is nowhere to run for shelter on the south side of the firth in strong northerly winds east of Granton, except perhaps close to HW, when Port Seton and Cockenzie would be accessible, if uncomfortable. Correspondingly, the approach to all harbours on the north side is hazardous in strong onshore winds.

Harbours authority

The Firth of Forth and the following individual harbours are controlled by Forth Ports plc: Leith, Granton, Grangemouth, Burntisland, Kirkcaldy, Methil.

Forth Navigation Service operates 24 hours on VHF Ch 71, as well as Ch 12 and 20 as working channels.

Tides

Streams in the firth east of Oxcars run generally at less than 1 knot, but may be faster where restricted.

The tidal constant throughout the outer part of the firth is within 15 minutes of Leith.

Dangers

Drying rocks extend up to ½M from the shore in places.

WNW of Dunbar, Wildfire Rocks extend ½M east from the northwest point of Belhaven Bay.

The passage south of Bass Rock is nearly a mile wide. Great Car, a reef extending over 3 cables from the mainland SSE of Bass Rock, is marked by a stone beacon 12m high with a cross topmark.

Craigleith, a detached rocky islet 51m high, lies about 2½M west of Bass Rock. Clear water lies up to ½M south of Craigleith, but many drying rocks lie inshore. However, a direct passage outside both the Lamb, 24m high, a mile west of Craigleith, and Fidra, 31m high with a white light beacon, clears these.

North Dog, a rocky patch lying more than a cable northwest of Fidra, rarely covers.

Fidra to Granton

South channel may provide a slightly more sheltered passage south of Inchkeith, in southerly winds, but rocks extend over ¾M southeast of Inchkeith, marked by *Herwit* green conical light buoy.

Shoals and reefs extend ½M NE of Leith, south of Inchkeith.

Craig Waugh N card light buoy about 1¾M southeast of Herwit buoy marks a submerged rock.

Fidra from NNE. Note rocks between the island and the shore

Leith Approach R can light buoy lies 3M WSW of *Herwit* buoy.

Granton Harbour entrance stands 1½M WSW of *Leith Approach* buoy.

North channel is well marked for the benefit of shipping to Grangemouth.

On the north shore at Kinghorn Ness, NNW of Inchkeith, detached rocks dry up to 1½ cables off shore, and the bay between Kinghorn Ness and Burntisland dries almost as far as Sandend green conical buoy.

Berween Elie Ness and Fife Ness many lobster pots are laid off the coast.

Principal lights

Bass Rock Fl(3)20s46m10M 241°-vis-107°
Fidra Fl(4)30s34m24M (partly obscured from east by Bass Rock, Craigleith and The Lamb)
Inchkeith Fl.15s67m22M
Elie Ness Fl.6s15m18M
Isle of May Fl(2)15s73m22M
Fife Ness Iso.WR.10s12m21/20M
North Carr buoy Q(3)10s.

North Berwick

⊕ on leading line and with Lamb and Fidra in line, 55°04'N 02°43'W

Temporary anchorage may be found in offshore winds; the small harbour is full of small fishing boats and local yachts, dries with a hard bottom, and is subject to swell.

A low-tide landing platform with steps is established NW of the NW harbour wall. Visitors moorings are laid off this platform.

Anchor clear of the visitors moorings, or at neaps or with a shoal-draught boat, further inshore, west of the harbour entrance.

Visitors berths may be available alongside the quay in the harbour.

Dangers and marks

The bay is obstructed with rocks leaving a passage about ½ cable wide on its east side.

Light

A fixed light at the west end of the northwest breakwater shows red to seaward.

Supplies

Water tap on southeast side of harbour, petrol and diesel, *Calor Gas*, shops, hotels, PO, telephone, in town.

Rail and Bus services to Edinburgh.

East Lothian YC ☎ 01620 892698.

North Berwick from NNE

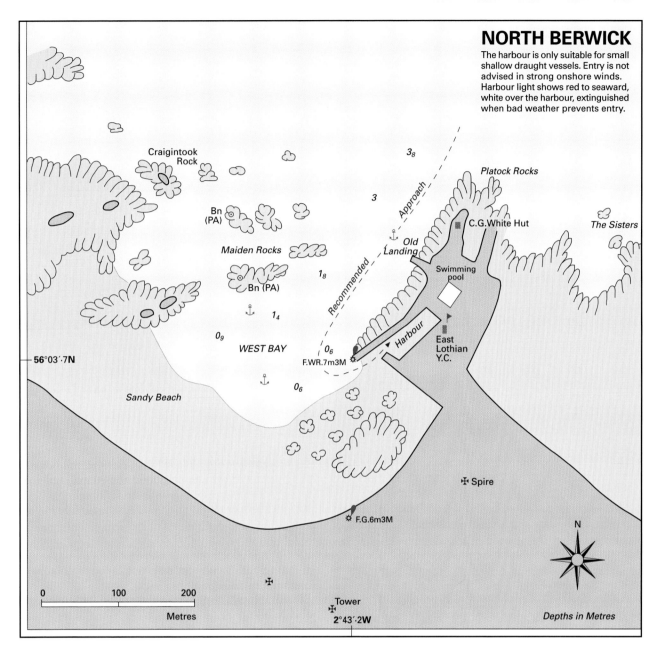

NORTH BERWICK
The harbour is only suitable for small shallow draught vessels. Entry is not advised in strong onshore winds. Harbour light shows red to seaward, white over the harbour, extinguished when bad weather prevents entry.

Port Seton

⊕ 55°58'·6N 02°57'·3W ¼M north of harbour entrance

A small drying harbour used by inshore fishing boats. The west harbour is rocky and unusable; the east harbour has a bottom of mud and sand, and is used by several inshore fishing boats. Rocks extend west and northeast from either side of the entrance, which almost dries.

Approach

From between NW and north.
Cockenzie and Port Seton Fishermen's Association
☎ 01875 811473.

Cockenzie

⊕ 55°58'·3N 02°58'W ¼M NNW of harbour entrance

The harbour lies immediately east of Cockenzie power station.

The west part has a rocky bottom and the part of the east harbour which dries least, inside the north breakwater, is 1·5m above chart datum.

Charts

BA *735* (1:25,000); Imray *C27* (plan); OS Landranger *66*.

Approach

From between northwest and northeast within two hours of HW.

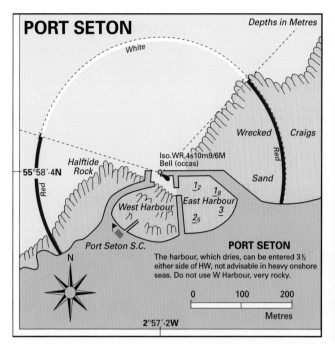

PORT SETON

Depths in Metres

White

55°58'·4N

Halftide Rock

Red

Wrecked   Craigs

Red

Iso.WR.4s10m9/6M
Bell (occas)

Sand

1_2

1_8
East Harbour
3

West Harbour

2_5

Port Seton S.C.

N

PORT SETON

The harbour, which dries, can be entered 3½ either side of HW, not advisable in heavy onshore seas. Do not use W Harbour, very rocky.

0   100   200

Metres

2°57'·2W

Fisherrow from NW

Port Seton

Fisherrow

⊕ 55°57'·3N 03°04'·4W ½M NNW of the harbour entrance

A fine stone harbour with a bottom of soft mud, the entrance of which dries 2·4m, approached across half a mile of drying sand, free from hazards apart from the occasional supermarket trolley or abandoned bicycle.

If space is available the crew of a yacht which can take the ground would find this a convenient place from which to visit Edinburgh.

Supplies

Water on quayside, petrol and diesel at garage, *Calor Gas*, shops, hotels, PO, telephone in town.

Harbourmaster ☎ 0131 665 5900.

Inchkeith

56°02'N 03°08'W

Shelter

From easterly winds may be had close to the mouth of a harbour on the west side of the island, but the proprietor imposes restrictions on landing.

Leith

⊕ 56°00'N 03°11'·5W close to approach buoy

In principle Leith is not available to yachts. Entrance is through a ship lock.

Forth Navigation Service operates 24 hours on VHF Ch 71.

Granton

⊕ 55°59'·5N 03°13'·1W ¼M north of harbour entrance

An artificial harbour built in the mid-19th century, much of it silted up so that yachts lie aground at all angles. Parts of the west harbour have been filled in for industrial development and it is an uninviting approach to a capital city. There are plans for extensive commercial and residential development.

Pontoons for visiting yachts (with security gated access) are provided on the east side of Middle Pier. Mooring is possible on the west side of the central quay at all states of tide alongside rather hostile piles.

Headquarters of Royal Forth Yacht Club and Forth Corinthian Yacht Club.

Tides

Tidal streams run strongly across the mouth of the harbour.

Dangers and marks

A beacon in Wardie Bay, east of harbour, marks a sewer outfall.

Lights

East breakwater head Fl.R.2s5m6M
Middle pier head F.R

Supplies

Water, diesel. Chandlery, *Calor Gas* at Seaspan, shops in town, PO, telephone.

There is an excellent stone slip for drying out, the bottom part of which is level, on the east side of middle pier.

Royal Forth YC ☎ 0131 552 8560
SeaSpan ☎ 0131 552 2224
CoSalt ☎ 0131 552 0011
Forth Corinthians YC ☎ 0131 552 5939
VHF Ch 37, 80.

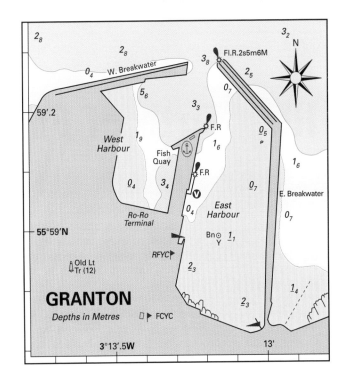

Granton Harbour from north

III. Firth of Forth: north

Burntisland

⊕ 56°03′N 03°14′W ¼M SSE of harbour entrance

A commercial harbour on the north shore of the firth, accessible at all states of tide, which may provide shelter for a visiting yacht. Access to enclosed dock is possible around HW – at a substantial cost.

In heavy weather there is a backwash off the breakwaters. Notes on a chart from 1730 claimed it was then the best harbour between London and Orkney, and recommended 'ships of burden' to drive in under full sail – on a rising tide – until they grounded.

Dangers and marks

Kirkbush Rock, awash, lies a cable off shore 3 cables east of the harbour entrance.

Drying reefs extend SSE from Lammerlaws Point at the east end of the harbour wall.

Lights

East breakwater Fl(2)G.6s7m5M
West breakwater Fl(2)R.6s7m

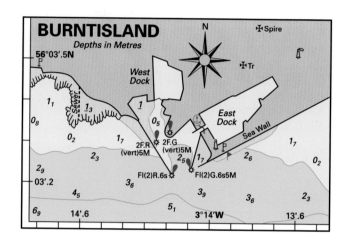

The 'boat shelter' inside the east point of the entrance is usually fully occupied by local boats but a mooring or alongside berth may be available. Visiting yachts should berth temporarily at the slip north of the entrance and report to HM's office east of the slip.

Burntisland harbour entrance

Kirkcaldy before it ceased to be a working port

Supplies

Water tap at sailing club, diesel, engineer, boatyard. *Calor Gas*, shops, hotels, petrol, PO, telephone in town. Boatyard at Starleyburn, 1M west of harbour.

Harbourmaster VHF Ch 12. Office on north quay ☎ 01333 426725

Kinghorn Yacht Services ☎ 01592 874581.

Kirkcaldy

⊕ 56°6'·6N 03°8'·8W 2 cables south of East pier head

A former commercial harbour, of which the outer part is shoal and the inner dock dries. No longer maintained, but small craft are moored in the old dock.

Dangers and marks

Drying sands and shoal water lie west of a line extending south from the entrance, and the approaches are silting.

Scares, a mile or so south of Kirkcaldy harbour.

A drying patch lies east of the east pier head. An unlit yellow beacon lies ½ cable southeast of the east pier head.

The least depth in the entrance is 0·2m.

Approach

Not within 2 hours of LW.

From east pass south of the yellow beacon.

From south keep the entrance bearing not less than 360°.

Lights

East pier Fl.WG.10s12m8M

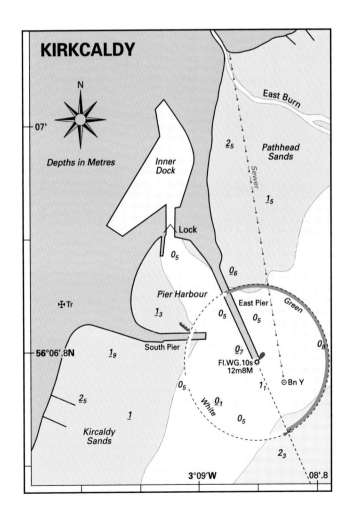

Dysart

⊕ 56°07'N 03°07'W close W of G buoy 3 cables off harbour entrance

The harbour is managed by Dysart Sailing Club, and provides a drying berth for visitors alongside a stone quay on the east side of the approach to the inner dock.

Dangers and marks

Rocks southeast of the entrance are marked by two starboard-hand buoys.

Methil

⊕ 56°10'·5N 03°0'·4W ¼M S of pier head.

Any port in a storm. A commercial harbour which does not cater for yachts but may provide shelter.

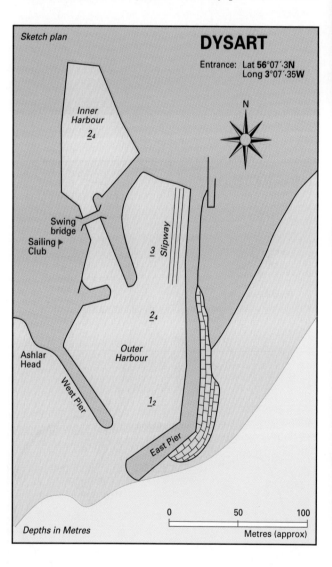

Sketch plan

DYSART

Entrance: Lat **56°07'·3N**
Long **3°07'·35W**

N

Inner Harbour

2₄

Swing bridge

Sailing Club

Slipway

3

Outer Harbour

2₄

Ashlar Head

West Pier

1₂

East Pier

0   50   100

Depths in Metres

Metres (approx)

Dysart

Dysart

Commercial traffic has declined, and only 70 ships were handled in 1999. It may be possible by prior arrangement to enter the enclosed dock.

Charts
BA *739* (1:10,000); Imray *C27;* OS Landranger *59*

Tides
Constant −0010 Leith (+0340 Dover)

Heights in metres

MHWS	MHWN	MTL	MLWN	MLWS
4·5	4·4	3·2	2·0	0·7

Dangers and marks
Sewer works ½M NW of harbour mouth marked by beacons.

Lights
Outer pier Oc.G.6s8m5M 280°-100°
Sewer works ½M NW Q.G

Harbourmaster VHF Ch 14. Office at east side of dock entrance
David Anderson Marine ☎ 01896 422400
Miller ☎ 01896 422694.

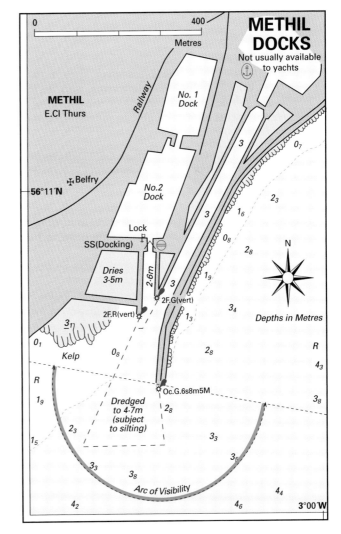

Methil

Elie

56°11'N 02°49'W

A stone breakwater on the north side of a promontory north of Elie Ness gives shelter to a couple of dozen yachts on drying trots, and drying berths are provided on the inside of the breakwater for visiting yachts which are able to take the ground.

Charts

BA *735* (1:25,000); Imray *C27* (plan); OS Landranger *59*. All harbours east of Elie are included in OS Explorer *371*

Dangers and marks

Elie Ness is marked by a white tower, 11m in height.
Drying reefs lie up to 2 cables from the head of Elie Bay.
At the west side of the bay detached rocks lie up to ¼M from Chapel Ness.
Of these Thill Rock, southeast of the point is marked by a red can light buoy, and East Vows, which dries 3·1m is marked by a beacon.

Lights

Elie Ness Fl.6s15m18M

Supplies

Water at toilets, petrol and diesel, hotel, PO, telephone in village.

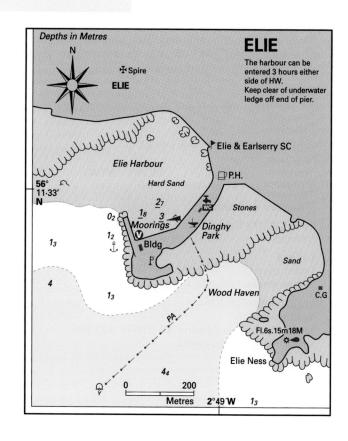

Depths in Metres

ELIE

The harbour can be entered 3 hours either side of HW.
Keep clear of underwater ledge off end of pier.

Elie

St Monance

56°12'N 02°46'W

The harbour dries completely.

Charts

BA *735* (1:25,000); Imray *C27* (plan); OS map *59*

Tides

Constant −0020 Leith (+0335 Dover)

Heights in metres

MHWS	MHWN	MTL	MLWN	MLWS
3·5	2·8	2·2	1·6	0·7

Dangers and marks

Drying reefs extend south on both sides of the entrance, with a subsidiary breakwater on the east side and a detached breakwater and a beacon on the west side.

Should not be approached in strong SE wind or NE swell.

Lights

East breakwater Oc.WRG.6s5m7-4M
East pier head 2F.G(vert)6m4M
West pier head 2F.R(vert)6m4M

At night

The lights at the entrance are sufficient guide.

Berth temporarily as convenient and consult harbourmaster.

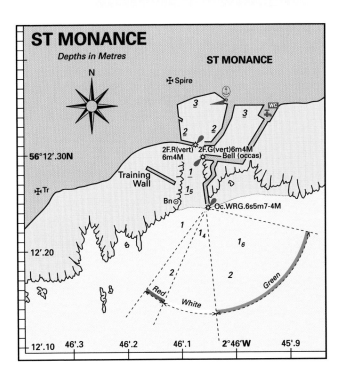

Supplies

Water, petrol at garage, diesel by tanker. *Calor Gas*, hotels, PO, telephone in village.

Harbourmaster ☎ 01333 730428. Office at middle pier.

St Monance

Pittenweem

56°12'N 02°44'W

An active fishing harbour but if the prawn fleet is away then yachts are made very welcome. Consult the harbourmaster on VHF before entering.

Charts

BA *735* (1:25,000); Imray *C27* (plan); OS Landranger *59*; OS Explorer *371*

Tides

Constant −0015 Leith (+0325 Dover)

Heights in metres

MHWS	MHWN	MTL	MLWN	MLWS
4·5	4·4	3·2		

Heavy scend with SE gales.

Dangers and marks

Drying rocks extend ½ cable south from the east breakwater and southwest from the west breakwater, marked by three unlit beacons, and a lit tripod beacon about 1 cable from the entrance.

The leading beacons are white columns with orange stripe, 3 and 10m high.

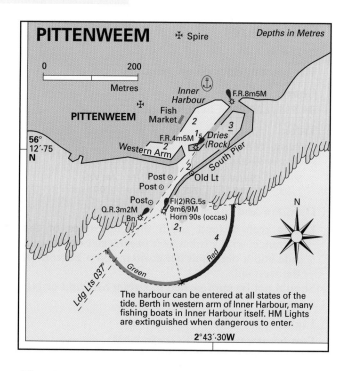

The depth in the entrance is 1·5m and the outer (east) harbour dries with a rocky bottom.

Approach

From southeast keep well off until the tripod beacon is identified and steer with it bearing not less than 300°, until the leading beacons are in line bearing 037° and steer on that bearing parallel to the line of beacons on the reef.

Lights

Outer beacon Q.R.3m2M
East breakwater head Fl(2)RG.5s9m6/9M
    Horn 90s(occas)
Ldg Lts F.R

Supplies

Water at western arm of Inner Harbour, petrol at garage, diesel by tanker, shops, hotel, PO, telephone in village. Chandlery: Fishermen's Mutual ☎ 01333 311263.

Harbourmaster ☎ 01333 312591 (office at north side of inner harbour).

Anstruther

⊕ on leading line 56°13'N 02°42'W

The Scottish Fisheries Museum is a feature of this harbour.

Charts

BA *735* (1:25,000); Imray *C27* (plan); OS Landranger *59*

Tides

Constant −0015 Leith (+0315 Dover)

Heights in metres

MHWS	MHWN	MTL	MLWN	MLWS
4·5	4·4	3·2	2·0	0·7

Pittenweem

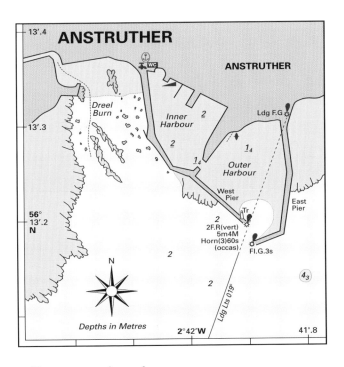

Anstruther, with the pontoons in the background

Dangers and marks

Drying reefs extend about a cable from shore. The harbour dries and the bottom of the outer harbour is hard sand and rock.

Lights

East pier head Fl.G.3s6m4M
West pier head 2F.R(vert)5m4M
Ldg Lts 019° F.G.11m4M lead into the harbour entrance

Supplies

Water at quays, petrol and diesel at garages (and by road tanker). *Calor Gas*, shops, PO, telephone, toilets and showers at HM office.

Harbourmaster VHF Ch 11. Office at northwest corner of inner harbour ☎ 01333 310836.

Crail

Probably the harbour which appears most often on calendars, Crail was one of Scotland's major trading ports in the 17th century.

There is one (drying) visitors berth alongside a quay.

Stone leading beacons, bearing 295°, lead into the drying approach channel, with a sharp turn to starboard into the harbour entrance which is 7m wide.

Anstruther, before the installation of pontoons

Approach to Crail harbour

Isle of May

56°11'N 02°33'W

The island is a National Nature Reserve, owned and managed by Scottish Natural Heritage.

Landing is only permitted at the Altarstones on the west side of the island and at Kirkhaven at the southeast end.

Kirkhaven, at the southeast of the island, is very confined but can be entered from northeast by bringing two white beacons in line, followed by two similar beacons at the head of the inlet. Prepare to clear out at once if the wind goes easterly.

Charts

BA *735* (1:25,000); Imray *C27*; OS Landranger *59*

Isle of May

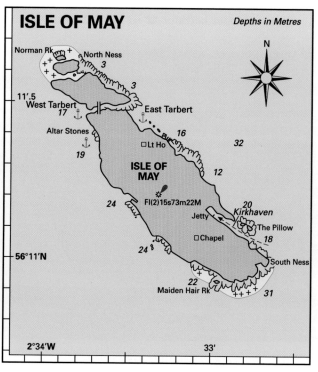

IV. Inner Forth Estuary

Passage west of Granton

Inchcolm, an island ¼M long on which stand the conspicuous ruins of an abbey, lies 6M west of Inchkeith, separated from the north shore by Mortimer's Deep, a channel half a mile wide, used by LPG tankers berthing at Braefoot Terminal.

Oxcars light beacon, white with a red band stands on a drying reef on the south side of the channel, ¾M SE of Inchcolm.

Granton gasholders, standing to the west of Granton Harbour, are conspicuous

Forth Bridge stands 9M west of Inchkeith.

Cramond Island, 2M west of Granton, stand on the edge of Drum Sand which dry out for a mile from the south shore.

Drum Sand continues west for 1½M to Hound Point, where a separate spit, Drum Sand, extends ENE, towards Inchmickery, a mile NNE of Cramond Island. The deepest water over Drum Flat is little more than 2m, about 3 cables west of Inchmickery.

Cow and Calves, a reef partly above water, lies 2 cables north of Inchmickery, and is separated from Cow and Calves by a channel ¼M wide.

Shoal banks lie up to 6 cables east of Oxcars and around Cow and Calves, so that without a large-scale chart the main channel has to be joined from the south either not less than a mile east of Oxcars or at a suitable rise of tide by taking the deepest water over Drum Flat.

At buoy *No.16* Drum Sand lies close to the south side of the channel.

Off Hound Point on the south shore is a detached tanker terminal used by very large vessels. The passage south of the terminal is 2 cables wide and may be used with care. Keep 500m off.

Long Craig Pier extends 2 cables from the south shore. Shoal water up to a cable further north of the pier extends west to the Forth Bridge.

Inchgarvie, a rocky island, lies on the east side of the Forth Rail Bridge; the main shipping channel is to the north. Shoal water extends up to 4 cables from the south shore between the bridges.

Hound Point, Oil Terminal and Forth Bridges

The main shipping channel

South of Inchcolm is well buoyed, beginning at *Fairway* buoy, about 4½M ENE of Inchkeith. Commercial vessels using this channel may be constrained by their draught.

Tides

Run at up to 3 knots through the main shipping channel north of Oxcars and close south of Inchcolm, although there is space for a yacht to navigate outwith the channel with care.

Passage in Mortimer's Deep, between Inchcolm and the north shore, is restricted owing to its use by large tankers serving Braefoot Terminal. Permission is required from Forth Navigation to enter Mortimers Deep.

Inchcolm

Labelled by the tourist brochures as 'the Iona of the East', the buildings of Inchcolm Abbey are more complete than most in Scotland and the island which is in the care of Historic Scotalnd is worth a visit.

Dangers and marks

Drying rocks extend 2 cables east and west of the island, and a cable northwest.

Meadulse Rocks, an extensive drying patch, lie north and northeast of the island, with an unmarked channel south of them. Car Craig, 9m high, stands at their east end, and a beacon stands a cable from their west end.

The Haystack, 6m high stands on a drying reef ½M west of Inchcolm.

Mortimer's Deep, which separates Inchcolm from the mainland, is used by LPG tankers serving Braefoot Terminal, and is well marked by light-buoys.

Approach

From west by Mortimer's Deep, taking care to avoid obstructing tankers. *No.14* west cardinal light buoy 3 cables west of the island and *No.10* red can light buoy, 1½ cables northwest of the island, mark the channel; the nearest rocks are about ¾ cable south of the line between these buoys. Keep at least ½ cable off the north point of the island and anchor north or northeast of the abbey, taking care to avoid a drying reef which extends from a point northeast of the abbey.

The approach from east is best avoided at low spring tide, as the passage south of Swallow Craig has less than 2m. From *No.13* green conical fairway buoy steer WNW to pass ½ cable north of Swallow Craig and anchor as before.

A wooden slip in the bay east of the abbey is sometimes used by tourist boats, and may also be used by yachts which can take the ground.

The quay should be left clear for tourist boats; also beware a low-water landing platform which dries.

Lights

No.14 west card buoy Q(9)15s

No.15 green con buoy Fl.G.6s, southwest of Inchcolm

No.9 green con buoy Q.G, close southeast of the Haystack

No.10 red can buoy Fl(2)R.5s

No.8 red can buoy Fl.R.2s, northwest of Meadulse Rocks

No.13 green conical buoy Fl.G.9s, east of Inchcolm

No facilities.

Inchcolm and the tanker terminal at Braefoot Bay. Swallow Craig at bottom right, and Meadulse Rocks above

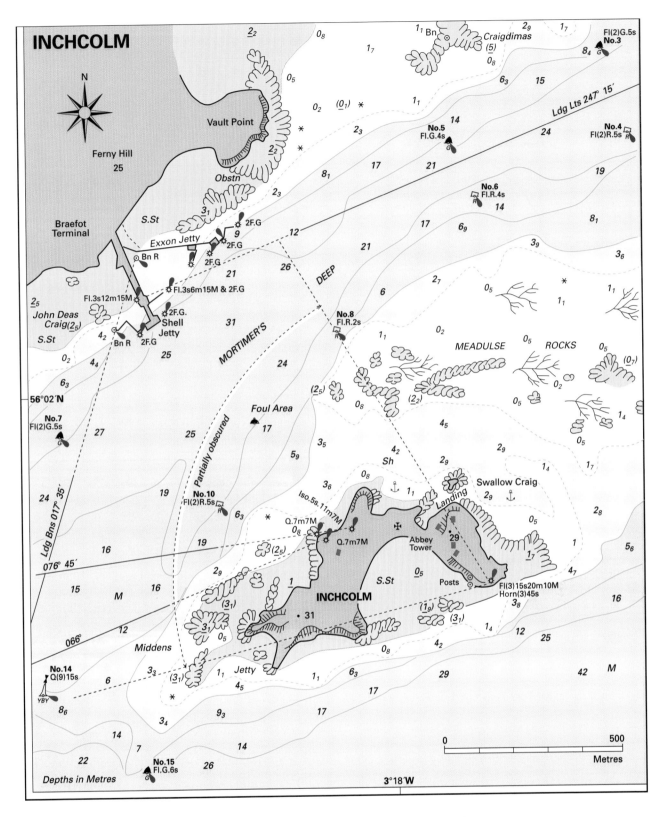

INCHCOLM

Aberdour

56°03'N 03°17'·7W

It may be possible to find a drying berth alongside the north side of the stone pier. Otherwise in offshore winds anchor south of a line joining the ruined pier on the east side of the bay and the sewer outfall beacon, and east of Little Craigs beacon.

Dangers and marks

The foreshore dries off for more than a cable south of the stone pier which shelters the drying harbour. A yellow beacon at the LW line at the west side of the bay marks a sewer outfall, and another beacon 2 cables further south stands on Little Craig, a detached rock awash at half tide.

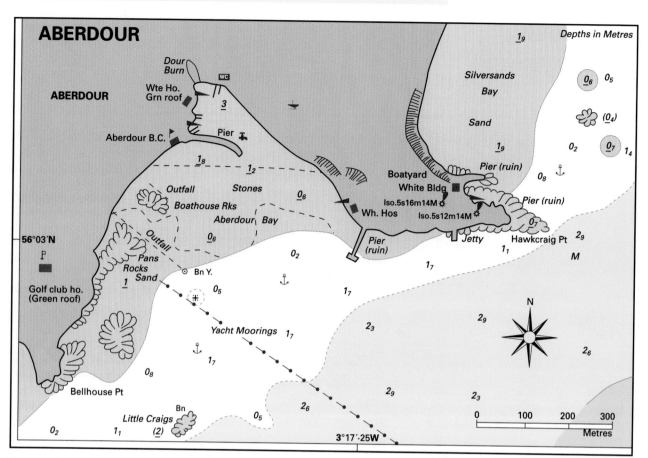

ABERDOUR

Depths in Metres

Dour Burn

ABERDOUR

Wte Ho.
Grn roof

WC

3

Aberdour B.C.

Pier

1_8

1_2

Outfall

Stones

Boathouse Rks

Aberdour Bay

0_6

0_6

56°03′N

0_6

Outfall

Pans
Rocks
Sand

1

0_2

Golf club ho.
(Green roof)

Bn Y.

0_5

Yacht Moorings

1_7

1_7

0_8

Bellhouse Pt

Little Craigs
(2)

Bn

0_5

0_2

1_1

3°17′·25W

Silversands
Bay

Sand

1_9

1_9

0_6 0_5

(0_4)

0_2

0_7 1_4

Boatyard
White Bldg
Iso.5s16m14M
Wh. Hos

Iso.5s12m14M

0_8

Pier (ruin)

Pier (ruin)

0_7

Pier
(ruin)

Jetty

1_7

1_1

Hawkcraig Pt

2_9

M

2_3

2_9

2_6

2_9

2_6

2_3

N

1_9

0   100   200   300
Metres

Aberdour Bay from southwest

Supplies

Water at harbour, petrol and diesel at village. Shop, hotel, PO, telephone at village. Trains, buses.

Cramond

⊕ 55°59'·9N 03°17'·3W on 2m contour north of Cramond Island

The river mouth on the south shore of the firth, which was used as a port by the Romans, as well as by sailing coasters in the 19th century, is approached by a drying channel about a mile long from the west side of Cramond Island.

This channel depends on local knowledge, although it is marked on the starboard side by a sequence of perches.

A stone sill just north of the village, intended to retain water for boats to stay afloat on moorings, is a trap for the unwary visitor.

It is possible to anchor in a pool close west of Seal Rock on the west side of Cramond Island. The depth on the Bar off the north end of the island is 0·2m.

Port Edgar

⊕ 56°00'·0N 03°24'·5W ¼M north of harbour entrance

A marina lies in an old naval harbour immediately west of the Forth Road Bridge.

Charts

BA *736* (1:15,000); Imray *C27* (plan); OS Landranger *65*

Tides

Tidal streams run strongly across the mouth of the harbour;
The west-going stream begins about –0530 Leith (+0150 Dover).
The east-going stream begins about +0030 Leith (+0430 Dover).

Heights in metres

MHWS	MHWN	MTL	MLWN	MLWS
4·8	4·7	3·3	2·2	0·8

Shelter

Is not so good as it appears. A floating barrier of old tyres helps to reduce the effects of swell and wash from passing ships, but the pontoons oscillate when there is any disturbance, and staff recommend that adjacent boats are moored with their bows in opposite directions to reduce the possibility of masts becoming entangled. The harbour is silting although attempts are made to keep a fairway clear.

Visitors berths on the north ends of the rows of pontoons are very vulnerable to wash and swell. No yacht should be left unattended at one of these berths; fenders have been burst and the topsides of a steel boat dented in this position.

Cramond Island from north-northwest

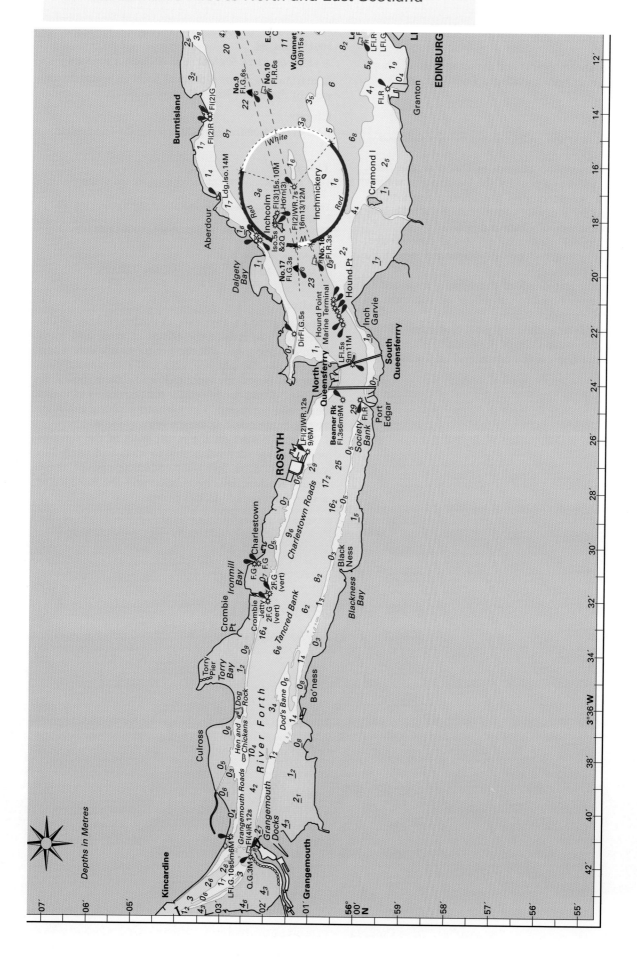

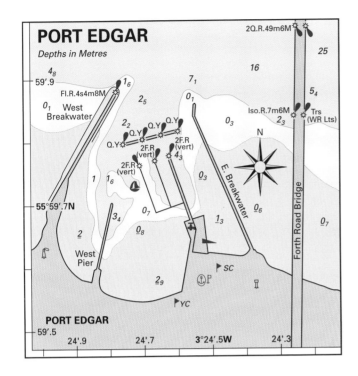

PORT EDGAR
Depths in Metres

Prior arrangements should be made for the use of a vacant berth as far inshore as possible, and mooring lines very carefully arranged to avoid damage.

A reef extends 20 metres west from the head of the east breakwater, so that the marina should only be approached by the west end of the tyre barrier, and the water is shoal near the barrier itself. A member of Port Edgar YC makes the following recommendation, 'For years there has been trouble if you sail anywhere near the tyre barrier. The safest way is to hug the west breakwater and then turn 090° along the line of the pontoon ends. Do not go near the tyres except at high water.'

Lights
West breakwater head Fl.R.4s4m8M (Dir 244°)
Q.Y mark the floating breakwater
2F.R(vert) mark each main pontoon

Port Edgar from southeast

Supplies
Water and electricity on pontoons. Diesel at head of concrete pier, by the crane. Fixed crane (5 tons). Chandlery, *Calor Gas*, supplies and repairs for electronics, engine and rigging. Telephone, shops, PO, at Queensferry village.

Bosun's Locker (chandlery) ☎ 0131 331 3875
Forth Area Marine Electronics ☎ 0131 331 4343
Harbour office VHF Ch 37, 80. Office E of root of concrete pier.

Upper Forth Estuary
The Forth is navigable for 10M west of Port Edgar to Grangemouth and Kincardine Bridge.

The foreshore above the Forth Bridges is very soft mud, known as 'sleech'.

Dangers and marks west of Port Edgar
Half a mile west of Port Edgar, two yellow poles mark a sewer outfall. A reef extends 120m north of the outer pole. This reef has caused extensive damage to local yachts.

Limekilns and Charlestown
Both of these harbours are accessible at half tide. Limekilns is the HQ of Forth Cruising Club; it is possible to berth at Capernaum Pier (right foreground in photo) or at the Town Pier (upper left).

Blackness from northeast

Charlestown from southeast

Limekilns and Brucehaven from southeast

The oldest part of Charlestown harbour dates from the 18th century. Once crowded with sailing coasters, the harbour is now completely silted up and surrounded by egregious 'executive' houses.

Yachts can take the ground in soft smelly mud. Both are fully detailed in the FYCA *Handbook*.

Blackness

The fine castle, with very ancient roots, mainly an eighteenth-century building, constructed by the Hanoverian crown to suppress the natives, is worth a visit. Boats able to take the ground can go alongside the stone pier at the head of the bay (not the ruined jetty at the castle) within two hours of high water.

Bo'ness

The full name of this ancient town is Borrowstounness; later submerged in mining and other industrial activity which has since departed. The town centre is being restored as a showpiece and tourist attraction. There is a preserved steam railway. A fine wet dock survives, surrounded by cleared land, but is currently unusable.

Grangemouth

Grangemouth Docks are used by commercial shipping and yachts are charged at deterrent rates, although there is a boatyard in the inner dock; in practice boats are usually lifted out by crane from River Carron.

River Carron runs alongside the north wall of the docks, and a stone training wall with stone beacons lies on the north side of the river channel. A light beacon stands on the head of the training wall, and a port-hand light buoy marks the southeast edge of the channel at the entrance.

Forth and Clyde Canal

The canal has been reopened for through navigation, accessible by a new sea lock from the River Carron, which is entered north of Grangemouth Docks, the old entrance through the docks having been filled in and built over.

Headroom is restricted to 3m, and a pontoon with a hoist 12m high has been provided in the River Carron, just down-river from Grangemouth Boat Club. The pontoon dries out on a relatively steep mud bank – indeed the river dries out completely at this point and access to the pontoon is available about 2 hours before and 1 hour after high water.

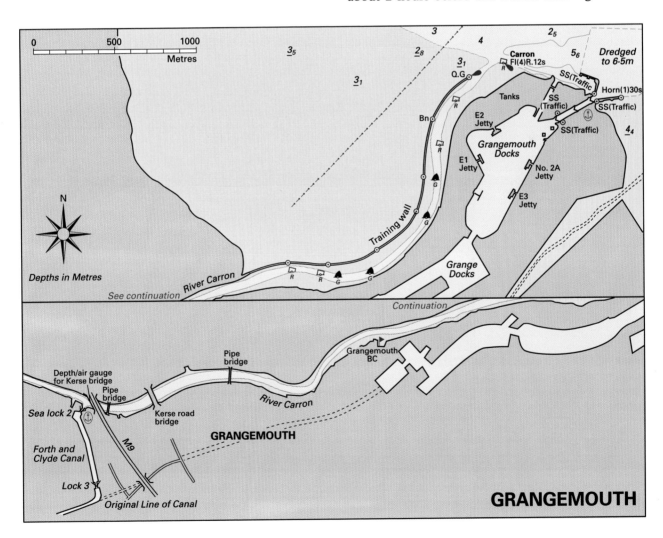

Depending on the tide, springs or neaps, and required draughts for the vessel, passage under the bridges may not be possible including a stop for demasting on one rising tide hence the options are to wait at the pontoon or proceed up river and anchor below the bridges until there is adequate clearance on the falling tide. Another option would be to move off the pontoon and wait for the next rising tide at the mooring piles in the river. Further developments are in hand/proposed. Alternatively, masts of sailing yachts can be lifted out at Port Edgar.

To arrange for a mast to be lifted out, call Steven Kelvin of FCS (Scotland) Ltd ☎ 01234 471535, mobile 07833 953 288. Timings will be flexible which will enable mast lift/lower operations outside the hours provided by Port Edgar; the facilities will appeal to those reluctant to put full trust in their auxiliary for the 10M passage up river. A hoist is provided at the west end of the canal.

Draught is limited to 1·5m; beam 6m, length 20m.

The canal is approximately 35M long, and rises by 20 locks over a distance of 10M to a summit level which is 17M in length, and then falls by way of a further 20 locks to Bowling, on the River Clyde.

A branch canal, the Edinburgh and Glasgow Union Canal is linked to the Forth and Clyde at the east end of the summit level by means of a giant lift, raising boats 25m, followed by a tunnel under the line of the Roman Antonine Wall and a new lock, to a single level running for 32M to Edinburgh.

The limiting dimensions of the Union Canal are expected to be: draught 1m, headroom 3m, beam 3·4m, length 20m.

These canals were closed in 1964 to facilitate construction of new roads and reopened in 2001.

River Forth

At a suitable rise of tide the very winding river is navigable a further 18M to Stirling.

Although of considerable historical interest there is little attraction in this part of the river. It is fully covered in the *FYCA Handbook*. BA chart *741* covers this river to Stirling.

Kincardine Bridge no longer opens, and headroom is 9m. Stirling is the limit of navigation, but several bridges below the town prevent boats with masts from reaching it.

The upper reaches of River Forth are navigable at high water to Stirling, at the bottom of this photo, at least to RIBs and shoal-draught boats

V. Fife Ness to Kinnaird Head

This section of coast, about 85M in extent, alternates between sand dunes and rocky cliffs. There is no natural shelter except for the Firth of Tay, which may be dangerous to enter in strong onshore winds.

For hundreds of years the Bell Rock, about 10M off shore, was a major hazard to shipping making for the Tay, until Robert Stevenson constructed the Bell Rock lighthouse in 1811.

This coast is a likely landfall for yachts from mainland Europe making for the Moray Firth or the Pentland Firth, and its few artificial harbours are of correspondingly significant importance.

Except in heavy onshore wind, the Tay may be convenient for a brief visit to Edinburgh and central Scotland by public transport.

For minor harbours see FYCA *Handbook*.

Charts

BA *190, 210, 213* (1:75,000), *1407, 1409* (1:200,000); Imray *C23* (1:250,000); OS Landranger *59, 54, 45, 38, 30;* OS Explorer *371, 382, 396, 406, 421, 427*

Dangers and marks

A yellow spherical Lt buoy 3 cables off shore, 8 cables S of Fife Ness lighthouse has no navigational significance.

At Fife Ness a low white lighthouse and the coastguard building stand on the headland.

North Carr reefs extend ½M NE from Fife Ness marked by a beacon.

North Carr E cardinal buoy lies nearly 2M ENE of Fife Ness.

Bell Rock lighthouse, a white tower 36m in height, stands on a drying reef 11M NE of Fife Ness.

Scurdie Ness, on the south side of the entrance to Montrose, is marked by a lighthouse 39m in height.

Dunnottar Castle ruins, a mile south of Stonehaven, stand conspicuously on a cliff top.

Girdle Ness lighthouse, at the south side of the entrance to Aberdeen harbour, is a white tower, 37m in height.

The Scares, a drying reef, extends 4 cables from the south point of Cruden Bay, about 7M south of Peterhead, marked by a port-hand light- and bell-buoy.

Buchan Ness lighthouse at the south side of Peterhead Bay, is a white tower with red bands, 35m in height.

Fife Ness to Buchan Ness

A yacht can safely pass inside *North Carr* buoy if the beacon is identified.

A passage from the vicinity of St Abb's Head to Arbroath and the coast further north would pass to the east of Bell Rock; a direct course from (or to) the Firth of Forth or Isle of May would normally pass west of it.

Closing the coast around Buchan Ness, look out for The Scares.

For passage beyond Buchan Ness see page 59.

Lights

North Carr light buoy Q(3)10s
Fife Ness LtHo Iso.WR.10s12m21/20M
Bell Rock LtHo Fl.5s28m18M
Scurdie Ness LtHo Fl(3)20s38m23M
Todhead LtHo Fl(4)30s41m18M
Girdle Ness LtHo Fl(2)20s56m22M
The Scares light buoy Fl.R.10s
Buchan Ness LtHo Fl.5s40m28M

St Andrews

56°20'·5N 02°46'W

Although historically a major trading port, the harbour is of only marginal use to a yacht on passage. The drying outer harbour is occupied by inshore fishing boats, and the inner harbour has gates which are usually left open. The town, with its castle and ancient university is of great interest.

Tide

Constant –0015 Leith (+0330 Dover)

Dangers and marks

A breakwater with a disused light beacon on its head stands on the north side of the entrance.

Drying reefs extend up to a cable NE of the breakwater head, with a detached beacon ½ cable east of it.

Burn Stools rocks on the south side of the entrance extend a cable ESE of the breakwater.

St Rule's Tower is conspic.

Approach

With the head of the breakwater in line with St Rule's Tower 280°.

No navigational lights.

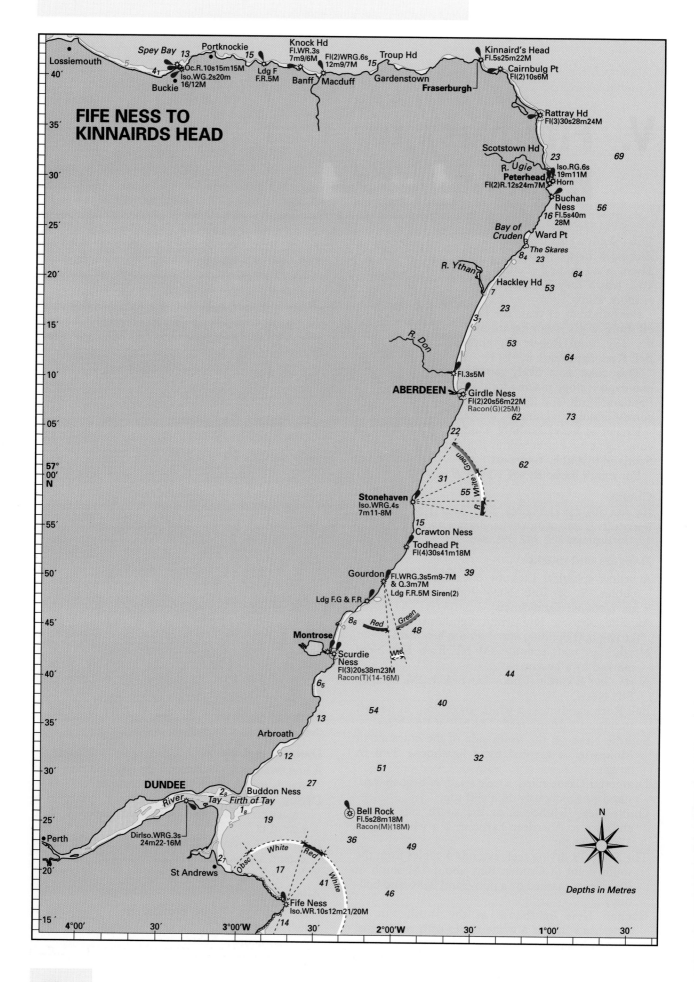

FIFE NESS TO
KINNAIRDS HEAD

Lossiemouth
40′
Spey Bay 13
Portknockie
15
Knock Hd
Fl.WR.3s
7m9/6M
Troup Hd
Gardenstown
Kinnaird's Head
Fl.5s25m22M
Cairnbulg Pt
Fl(2)10s6M
Oc.R.10s15m15M
Buckie
Iso.WG.2s20m
16/12M
Ldg F
F.R.5M
Banff Macduff
Fl(2)WRG.6s
12m9/7M
15
Fraserburgh
35′
Rattray Hd
Fl(3)30s28m24M
30′
Scotstown Hd
23
69
R. Ugie
Peterhead
Fl(2)R.12s24m7M
Iso.RG.6s
19m11M
Horn
25′
Buchan
Ness
16 Fl.5s40m
28M
56
Bay of
Cruden
Ward Pt
The Skares
8₄ 23
20′
R. Ythan
Hackley Hd 53
7
64
23
3₁
53
15′
64
R. Don
10′
Fl.3s5M
ABERDEEN
Girdle Ness
Fl(2)20s56m22M
Racon(G)(25M)
62
73
05′
22
Green
57°
00′
N
31
White
55
62
55′
Stonehaven
Iso.WRG.4s
7m11-8M
R.
15
Crawton Ness
Todhead Pt
Fl(4)30s41m18M
50′
Gourdon Fl.WRG.3s5m9-7M
& Q.3m7M
Ldg F.R.5M Siren(2)
39
Ldg F.G & F.R
8₆ Red
Green
45′
Montrose
48
Scurdie
Ness
Fl(3)20s38m23M
Racon(T)(14-16M)
Wte
44
6₅
40′
40
54
35′
13
Arbroath
32
12
51
30′
DUNDEE
27
2₈ Buddon Ness
River Tay Firth of Tay
1₈
19
Bell Rock
Fl.5s28m18M
Racon(M)(18M)
36
49
25′
Perth
Dirlso.WRG.3s
24m22-16M
27
White
Red
N
Obsc
17
White
46
20′
St Andrews
41
Depths in Metres
15′
Fife Ness
Iso.WR.10s12m21/20M
14
4°00′
30′
3°00′W
30′
2°00′W
30′
1°00′
30′

Shelter

Marginal except in drying inner harbour.

Supplies

Water at inner harbour, petrol and diesel at garages. *Calor Gas*, shops, PO, telephone, hotels in town.

River Eden, 2M north of St Andrews, is shoal, with a peripatetic bar at the entrance and an RAF airfield on its north bank.

Between the Eden and the Firth of Tay the shore is low-lying and wooded.

Firth of Tay

Charts

BA *1481* (1:25,000); OS Landranger *54*

The Firth of Tay is a broad shallow river estuary with drying banks on either side of the fairway, and a bar on which the tide and wind are often in conflict. The estuary is used by very large tankers, oil rig supply vessels, and even occasionally by oil rigs.

The fairway is entered between Buddon Ness, 56°28'N 02°44'W, a low sandy point on which stand two stone towers (disused leading beacons), and Tentsmuir Point, about 3M SW.

The channel, ½M wide, lies between Gaa Sand which extends 1½M east from Buddon Ness on the north side of the estuary and Abertay Sands which extend further eastward on the south side of the channel.

The position of the sands varies, and although The Bar, 1½M further east, has a depth of 6m, any sea from the east especially in combination with an ebb tide creates severe conditions there.

The fairway is marked by buoys which are altered to suit changes in the channel, and although there are large areas outwith the fairway with enough

depth for a yacht, drying banks and unmarked obstructions lie close to the line of buoys at some points. At the time of writing the buoys are as follows – all port-hand light buoys unless otherwise noted:

Fairway RWVS buoy lies about 4M eastward from Buddon Ness, with two lateral light buoys on the east side of the bar a mile WSW.

Abertay east cardinal light buoy, 1½M further WSW, marks the east end of Gaa Sand, with *Abertay* light buoy ¼M south of it.

The channel is further marked by *Inner* light buoy; *South Lady* light buoy with *North Lady* starboard-hand light buoy on the north side.

Pool buoy lies north of Tentsmuir Point and *Horseshoe* south cardinal light buoy a mile further west on the north side of the channel with a yellow conical light buoy about 3 cables ENE of it. *Scalp* light buoy lies another mile further west, with *Larick* disused pile light beacon beyond it, and the entrance to Tayport harbour beyond that.

At this point, about 8M from *Abertay* buoy, the firth is ¾M wide, between Broughty Castle on the north side, and Tayport on the south side. *Craig* buoy, near mid channel, and *Newcome* buoy 4 cables NW may be disregarded by yachts, but shoals and drying banks extend up to 1½ cables from the south shore in places.

Tay Road Bridge lies 2M west of *Craig* buoy.

Tay Railway Bridge lies 2M west of the road bridge, and the river is navigable by small coasters towards the top of the tide by a tortuous channel a further 16M to Perth.

A chart of the river beyond the railway bridge, formerly published by Tay Estuary Research Centre, University of Dundee, is no longer available.

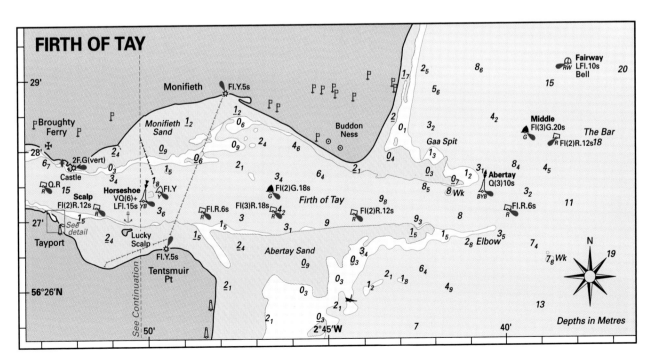

Tayport

Tides

In the channel south of Buddon Ness

The in-going stream begins about −0540 HW Leith (−0155 Dover).

The out-going stream begins about +0020 HW Leith (+0405 Dover).

Constant −0000 Aberdeen (+0338 Dover)

Heights in metres

MHWS	MHWN	MTL	MLWN	MLWS
4·2	4·2	3·0	1·9	0·7

Approach

Visiting yachts should call port control on Ch 16 or

12 (24hrs) to avoid the risk of obstructing commercial traffic.

From any direction make for *Middle* buoys and steer WSW for *Abertay* then west to pick up channel buoys in sequence.

Although the chart shows swatchways through Abertay Sands these change frequently and there is almost always broken water over the sands, for which reason they were a favourite spot for SAR helicopter training. They should not be attempted by strangers.

Lights

Fairway LFl.10s
Middle (S) Fl(2)R.12s
Middle (N) Fl(3)G.20s
Abertay E Car Q(3)10s
Abertay Fl.R.6s
Inner Fl(2)R.12s
South Lady Fl(3)R.18s
North Lady Fl(3)G.18s
Pool Fl.R.6s
Horseshoe VQ(6)+LFl.15s
Scalp Fl(2)R.12s
Craig Q.R
Newcome Fl.R.6s
Tayport High LtHo DirIso.WRG.3s24m22-16M

At night

Identify the *Middle* buoys and pass between them, steer SW to pass between *Abertay* buoys then keep in the white sector of Tayport High Light until *Scalp* buoy, and steer for *Craig* buoy or your chosen anchorage.

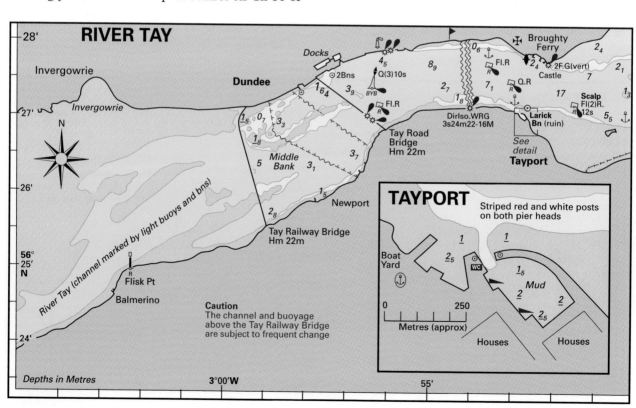

Anchorages and moorings

Broughty Ferry

56°28'N 02°52'W

Broughty Castle is conspicuous.

A rock awash lies about a cable off, and in line with, the NW pier.

Rocks, which cover at HW, extend from the south face of the SE pier.

The small drying harbour is accessible after half flood. The SE side has a good masonry wall. On the NW side lies a long sloping ramp (originally access for a rail ferry to Tayport before the Rail Bridge was built).

The castle was built on the site of a much older one, to protect the Tay from Russian invasion at the time of the Crimean War. It now contains an excellent museum featuring the local fishing and whaling industry.

Royal Tay Yacht Club, half a mile west of Broughty Castle, welcomes visitors, and can usually provide a mooring. ☎ 01382 477516.

In strong SW wind an alternative anchorage is at Woodhaven, or berth in Tayport harbour.

Tayport

56°27'N 02°53'W

The harbour has been dredged by the Tayport Boat Owners' Association, but still dries, soft mud.

Larick pile beacon, ¼M east of the harbour entrance marks the north edge of a drying bank.

The west side of the approach is marked by small pink buoys. Berth on the north wall and pay dues at the harbour café.

Supplies

Water, shops PO, telephone.

Woodhaven

56°26'N 02°58'W

Stands on the south shore between the bridges, off a stone slip. This is the best anchorage in SW wind. Anchor clear of moorings.

Dundee

56°28'N 02°57'W

A Victorian commercial and industrial city, once dependent mainly on jute and whaling, and in earlier times one of the principal harbours for Scotland's overseas trade. The city has now rebuilt its fortunes around the oil and electronics industries and half of its wet docks have been filled in.

Because the town's shipbuilders were familiar with Antarctic conditions, the polar research ship *Discovery* was built there, and has now been returned to the city to provide the centrepiece of a lavish audiovisual display.

Unicorn, the oldest ship afloat in Britain, is being restored in the dock at Dundee.

The first Tay Railway Bridge, built in 1878, collapsed spectacularly the following year, and was commemorated by possibly the worst poet in the English language, William McGonagall. The bridge was replaced and continues in use.

Fowler and Beacon Rocks, marked by beacons and an unlit port-hand buoy, lie SW of the dock entrance.

Rocks and shoals extend 2 cables from the shore below the road bridge.

A good mark for the dock entrance is a gasholder to the north of it.

Anchoring is prohibited off the docks and wharves as far out as a line extending east from Beacon Rock.

The gates to the enclosed docks normally open two hours before HW and close ½ hour before HW. A yacht intending to enter the docks must call port control (Ch 16 or 12) at least two hours in advance; an appropriate time is on passing the fairway buoy.

Berth temporarily at steps in masonry wall on the east side of the dock entrance. It is also possible to berth at a piled wharf outside the dock entrance, although this would not be a suitable berth at which to remain overnight.

There are no lights at the dock entrance.

Chandlery 'Sea and Shore', Victoria Dock.

Harbourmaster VHF Ch 12, ☎ 01382 224121. Office at NW corner of Victoria (west) Dock.

Between the bridges, Middle Bank lies 4 cables from the north shore joined to the shore by shoals and drying banks ½M east of the railway bridge.

Underwater cables cross the river west of a line ½M SW of the road bridge.

Anchor off the slip at the west side of Craig Harbour, 2 cables west of the road bridge.

For the passage up the river to Perth, see FYCA *Handbook* and OS Explorer *380*.

Any commercial traffic will be moving – either up or down river – during the two hours before HW, especially at Springs.

There may be no space at Perth at which to moor; call the harbourmaster on VHF Ch 09, ☎ 01738 624056 before committing to passage.

Arbroath

⊕ 56°33'N 02°34'W, on leading line ½M ESE of entrance

A fishing harbour which dries inside the entrance. Drying rocks lie on either side of the approach up to ¼M from the entrance. Any sea from SE breaks heavily in the entrance channel.

A white tower at the head of the entrance channel, formerly used for signalling to Bell Rock lighthouse, is conspicuous.

White leading beacons, close east of the tower, bearing 299°, lead between the rocks to the entrance.

A sewer outfall is marked by a Y spherical light buoy ½M south of the west pier head.

Another sewer outfall is marked by a yellow light beacon ½ cable SSE of the west pier head.

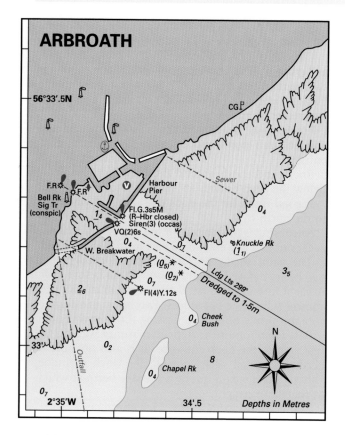

Supplies

Water, electricity points on quay, chandlery (Arbroath Fishermen's Association), boatyard. petrol and diesel. *Calor Gas*, shops, PO, telephone, hotels in town.

Harbourmaster ☎ 01241 872166. Office at north side of former wet dock.

Arbroath was the shore station for the Bell Rock lighthouse, and there is a small museum in the old signal tower. Before the lighthouse was built, under the supervision of Robert Stevenson between 1807 and 1811, the Abbot of 'Aberbrothock' (Arbroath) had a bell set up on the Inchcape Rock, its original name, which inspired an epic ballad by Robert Southey with that title.

Arbroath is also famous in Scottish history for the Declaration of Arbroath in 1341, a document which stands alongside Magna Carta and the American Declaration of Independence in the development of democracy.

The coast between Arbroath and Montrose consists of cliffs and rolling hills.

Lunan Bay, 3M south of Girdle Ness is suitable for anchorage in offshore winds.

Montrose

⊕ ½ cable N of red buoy 56°42'·2N 02°25'·4W

The harbour is used by general cargo and oil rig supply vessels throughout the day and night. The tide in the River Esk runs at up to 8 knots as it fills and empties the tidal Montrose Basin, above the bridge.

The entrance channel runs between Scurdie Rocks, which extend 2 cables east of Scurdie Ness on the south side, and Annat Sands on the north side. Seas break heavily on Annat Sands with an onshore wind especially when opposed by an ebb tide.

Scurdie Ness lighthouse is conspicuous.

Charts

BA *1438* (1:7,500); Imray *C23* (plan); OS Landranger *54*

Tides

The in-going stream begins about –0520 HW Aberdeen
  (–0300 Dover).
the out-going stream begins about +0055 HW Aberdeen
  (+0315 Dover).
Constant +0055 Aberdeen (+0320 Dover)

MHWS	MHWN	MTL	MLWN	MLWS
4·8	3·9	2·8	1·9	0·7

Dangers and marks

Scurdie Rocks extend 2 cables east from Scurdie Ness and a port-hand light buoy lies 2 cables further east.

A green conical light buoy lies 2 cables north of the port-hand buoy. A green conical light buoy marks the edge of Annat Bank NE of the lighthouse.

Conspicuous white towers on the north shore in line bearing 271·5° are leading marks for the outer part of the channel.

Most of the harbour dries, except for a small part of the SW corner, and the gates of the former West Dock have been 'away' for many years. The dock gates are to be restored and pontoons installed, probably by summer 2004.

Charts

BA *1438* (1:12,500); Imray *C23* (plan); OS Landranger *54*

Tides

Constant +0450 Aberdeen (–0320 Dover)
Heights in metres

MHWS	MHWN	MTL	MLWN	MLWS
4·0	4·1	2·4	1·8	0·7

The entrance channel has been dredged to 1·5m below CD as far as the NW head of the quay on the NE side of the entrance.

Approach

Only within 3 hours of HW, on the line of the leading beacons 299°, and only if no sea is breaking on shore. Look out for fishing vessels coming out; follow round to starboard, secure temporarily and consult harbourmaster.

Lights

Outfall buoy Fl.Y.3s
Outfall beacon Fl(4)Y.12s
NE side of entrance Fl.G.3s8m5M Siren(3)60s(occas)
SW side of entrance VQ(2)6s6m4M
Ldg Lts 299° F.R

Yacht berths in SW corner.

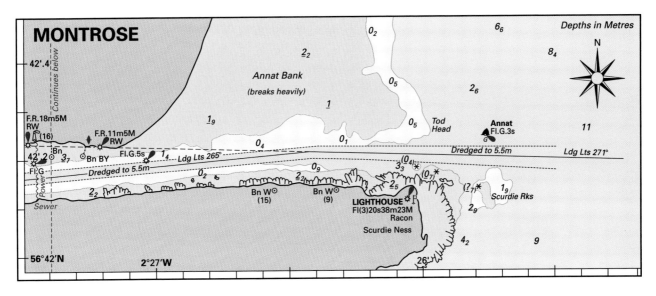

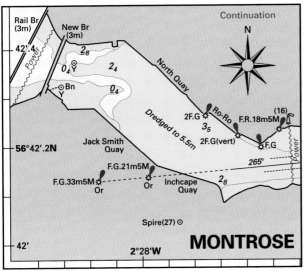

Less conspicuous lattice towers with orange triangle topmarks on the south shore in line bearing 265° are leading marks for the inner channel.

Approach from any direction keep at least a mile off shore until on the leading line. Call Montrose Harbour Radio before entering, otherwise make fast temporarily at the pilot berth (on the north bank) to consult the harbourmaster. Quays on the south shore are used by oil rig supply vessels.

Berth at the west end of River Quay on the north side, but note that the water is shoal for ½ cable SE of a projecting stone quay. The north quay consists of sheet piling with an overhanging concrete deck under which guard rails could catch as the tide rises; it is preferable to berth outside another vessel if possible.

If you have to enter against the ebb, it's as well to be aware that there may be a strong eddy close to the quay, which can foul up the most meticulously planned approach.

There used to be an excellent wet dock on the north bank which has been filled in to provide space for warehouses.

Lights

Scurdie Ness LtHo Fl(3)20s38m23M
Scurdie Rocks red can buoy Q.R
Annat Bank outer green conical buoy Q.G
Annat (inner) Fl.G.3s
Ldg Lts 271·5° F.R.11m5M
Beacon beside rear leading light Fl.G.5s
Ldg Lts 265° F.G.21m5M

At night

Identify the outer buoys, pass between them, pick up and follow the leading lights in sequence.

Supplies

Water, diesel by road tanker (ask HM). *Calor Gas*, shops, PO, telephone, hotels.

Harbourmaster VHF Ch 12. Office at east end of North Quay.

The ruins of Dunnottar Castle are conspicuous a mile south of Stonehaven.

Johnshaven
56°47'N 02°20'W

About 2½M SSW of Gourdon, is a similar artificial harbour, but less accessible and less convenient.

Leading line 316° leads between reefs to the entrance.

Water, electric points on quayside.

Lights

Ldg Lts *Front* F.R *Rear* F.G (R when unsafe to enter)

Gourdon
56°49'N 02°17'W

An artificial harbour which dries, about half way between Montrose and Stonehaven.

The inner dock is protected in heavy weather by storm gates which allow water, but not waves, to pass through (i.e. it is not a wet dock) and boats take the ground.

In quiet weather a yacht can lie afloat just inside the south side of the entrance at LW.

Gourdon   *(Photo: former Grampian Regional Council)*

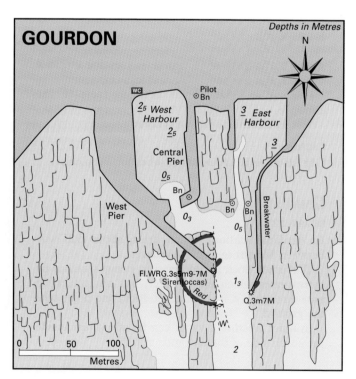

Charts

BA *210* (1:75,000); OS Landranger *45*

Tides

Constant +0035 Aberdeen (+0300 Dover)

Heights in metres

MHWS	MHWN	MTL	MLWN	MLWS
4·6	3·7	2·7	1·7	0·7

Dangers and marks

Reefs run out in a southerly direction (see photo). A perch stands on a reef on the west side of the entrance.

White cylindrical leading beacons, not easily distinguished, but lit at night, in line bearing 358°, lead to the entrance.

Approach

On the line of the beacons, turn to port round the west pier, looking out for vessels coming out. Make fast wherever the tide allows and make contact with harbourmaster.

Lights

W pier Fl.WRG.3s5m9-7M 344°-W-354°
E breakwater Q.3m7M
Ldg Lts F.R.5m5M (shows G when unsafe to enter)

Gourdon

At night
Approach in the W sector of W pier light or on leading lights and enter harbour as above.

Supplies
Water, petrol and diesel. *Calor Gas*, shop, PO, telephone, hotel. Marine engineer
Harbourmaster ☎ 01569 762741.
Note A 'Rover' ticket allowing unlimited use of harbours owned by Aberdeenshire and Moray and Banff Councils during a period of one week after the first entry is available at a charge of £10. In this chapter Johnshaven, Gourdon and Stonehaven are included, and many harbours in the following chapter.

Catterline
56°53'N 02°12'W

A mile north of Todhead, is a pleasant occasional anchorage in settled weather, but not a secure overnight anchorage.

Stonehaven
56°57'N 02°12'W

A pleasant harbour with many resident yachts. Shelter in the outer harbour is poor, but a small dredged berth is available on the east side of the inner basin if not already occupied, and a drying berth may usually be found.

Charts
BA *1438* (1:12,500), *210* (1:75,000); OS *45*

Stonehaven Harbour

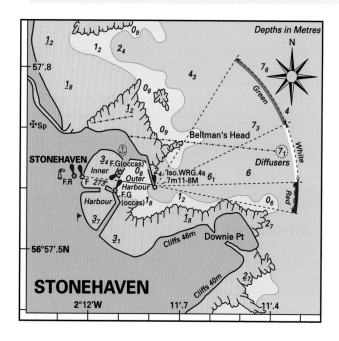

STONEHAVEN

Depths in Metres

Tides

Constant +0010 Aberdeen (+0235 Dover)
Heights in metres

MHWS	MHWN	MTL	MLWN	MLWS
4·5	3·6	2·6	1·7	0·6

Dangers and marks

Drying reefs extend up to a cable off shore south of Downie Point, south of the harbour, and up to ¼M north of the harbour. Heavy seas break at the entrance in strong onshore winds.

The entrance may not be easy to distinguish, particularly from the north.
A drying reef occupies much of the southwest side of the outer harbour.

Approach

On a bearing between 240°and 265°, and secure on the west side of the outer breakwater. If there is some swell consult the harbourmaster and enter the inner harbour when the tide has risen sufficiently; a small pool has been excavated against the east wall of the south inner harbour.

Lights

Breakwater head Iso.WRG.4s7m11-8M

At night

Approach in the white sector of the breakwater light; pass round the breakwater head.

Supplies

Water, electricity, petrol and diesel at garage (and by tanker). *Calor Gas*, shops, telephone, hotel, swimming pool.
Harbourmaster VHF Ch 11 or ☎ 01569 762741. Office at north side of inner harbour. Aberdeen and Stonehaven YC ☎ 01224 315486.

Minor anchorages

There are anchorages suitable for occasional daytime use in offshore or settled weather as below. For each of these the FYCA *Handbook* should be consulted.

Aberdeen

Newtonhill
57°02'N 02°08'W

Portlethen
57°03'N 03°06'W

Cove
57°06'N 02°05'W

Aberdeen

57°08'N 02°05'W

A major commercial port with no specific provision for yachts, although they are usually courteously received. Berths for oil rig service vessels are often in such short supply that others are waiting outside until a berth is free.

Charges are set at a level which does not encourage yachts, although one payment covers a stay of up to 5 days.

Charts
BA *1446* (1:15,000/1:7,500); Imray *C23* (plan); OS Landranger *38*

Tides
Constants – Aberdeen is a Standard Port
Heights in metres

MHWS	MHWN	MTL	MLWN	MLWS
4·3	3·4	2·5	1·6	0·6

Dangers and marks
Girdle Ness lighthouse, ½M SE of the entrance, is conspic. Drying rocks extend 2 cables seaward from Girdle Ness.

Approach
Call *Aberdeen Harbour Radio* before approaching; otherwise be ready for instructions by loudhailer from the control tower on the north side.

A yacht will probably be asked to come alongside Lower Jetty temporarily, just west of the control tower. Yachts are usually directed to berth alongside a floating linkspan for a roll-on ferry at Pacific Wharf on the north side of Albert Basin, the middle of the three dock basins.

Before leaving call Harbour Control and be prepared to wait to avoid hindering larger vessels.

Lights
Girdle Ness LtHo Fl(2)20s56m22M
North pier head Oc.WR.6s11m9M In fog F.Y Bell(3)12s
South breakwater head Fl(3)R.8s23m7M
Old South breakwater Q.R
South jetty Q.R
Elbow, north pier Oc.G.4s5m4M
Lower jetty at control tower Q.G
Ldg Lts 236° *Front* F.R.14m5M *Rear* F.R.19m5M

At night
Traffic signals are displayed at North Pier; a green light means entry is prohibited.

Supplies
Water by arrangement at fish market, petrol from garage; diesel by road tanker. *Calor Gas*, hotels, shops, PO nearby, public telephone within harbour area.

Rail, bus station nearby. Airport 10M.

Ship Chandler (Cosalt) ☎ 01224 588327
Aberdeen Boat Centre ☎ 01224 631631
BCA Services ☎ 01224 582800
Coastguard ☎ 01224 592334
Harbourmaster VHF Ch 12, 10, 11, 13. ☎ 01224 592571. Office at north side of Victoria Dock.

Minor anchorages
(see *FYCA Handbook*)

Ythan Estuary
57°18'N 01°59'W

A shallow river winding through dunes, with a bar at the entrance the position of which varies.

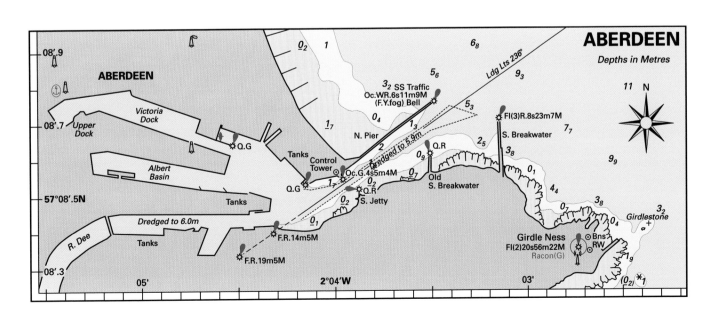

Collieston

57°25'N 01°51'W

Port Errol

57°25'N 01°51'W

A drying artificial harbour in the NW corner of Cruden Bay. Berthing master ☎ 01779 812673.

The Skares, a reef extending 3½ cables from the south point of Cruden Bay, is marked by a port-hand light buoy 7 cables off shore.

Boddam

57°28'N 01°37'W

In most circumstances a passage-making yacht looking for a harbour would make for Peterhead, but Boddam is one of the few small harbours on this coast which does not dry out.

Charts, tides

As Peterhead.

Dangers and marks

Buchan Ness lighthouse, about ¼M south of the harbour, is very conspic.

Meikle Mackie, a rocky islet 17m high, lies 50m east of the entrance.

The Skerry lies a further ¼M NNE, with submerged and drying rocks between the two islets and up to a cable north of the Skerry.

Drying rocks lie between Meikle Mackie and the shore south of the harbour entrance as well as ½ cable to the north.

A retaining wall lies across the harbour, the inner side drying, on the outer side the least depth is 1·5m.

Approach

North and west of Meikle Mackie.

Lights

None.

Shelter

Excellent once inside.

Supplies

Shop, pub.

Peterhead

⊕ close N of leading line 2 cables SE of breakwater head
57°29'·7N 01°46'W

The massive breakwater which completely shelters Peterhead Bay, the first maritime public work in Scotland on such a large scale, was built by the inmates of Peterhead prison at the beginning of the 20th century.

A marina lies in the SW corner of the bay, behind Princess Royal Jetty.

Charts

BA *1438* (1:20,000), *213* (1:75,000); Imray *C23* (1:250,000); OS Landranger *30*

Peterhead. Bay Marina

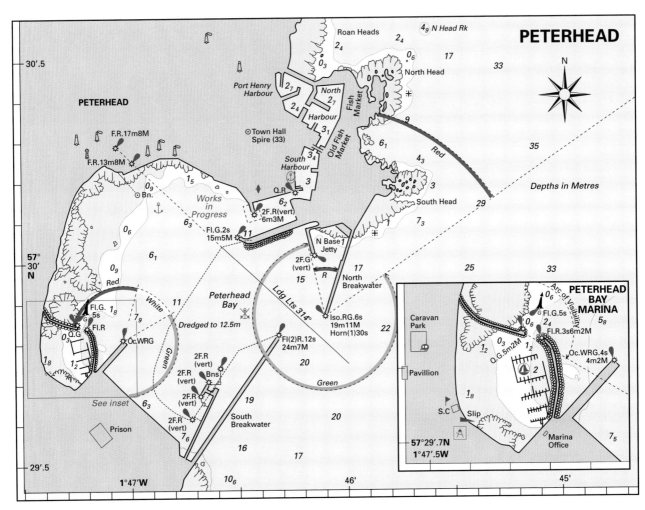

Tides

Constant −0000 Aberdeen (+0338 Dover)

Heights in metres

MHWS	MHWN	MTL	MLWN	MLWS
3·8	3·1	2·3	1·5	0·5

Dangers and marks

The entrance to Peterhead Bay is clear but there is heavy traffic, of fishing and oil supply vessels.

Backwash occurs off the north breakwater in heavy onshore weather.

Approach

To avoid conflict with commercial traffic, yachts approaching or leaving the Bay must call Peterhead Harbour on VHF Ch 14.

Peterhead Bay Marina is in the SW corner of the bay. Drying rocks extend up to a cable from the west side, marked by an E cardinal buoy at the entrance. to the marina. This buoy must be approached from east of north and left to starboard.

Lights

N breakwater Iso.RG.6s19m11M Horn 30s
S breakwater head Fl(2)R.12s24m7M
Princess Royal Jetty head Oc.WRG.4s4m2M 020°-R-195°-W-240°-G-020°
Marina east breakwater Fl.R.4s2M
Buoy Fl.G.5s
Marina west breakwater Q.G.2M

Supplies

Water at marina, diesel at Princess Royal Jetty, gas, shops, PO, telephone, hotel.

All services of a major fishing harbour (engineering, hull repairs, electronic, chandlery, are available in the harbour on the north side of the bay.

It is best to make an initial inspection by land from marina; If approaching harbour by boat call up harbour control on VHF first.

Harbourmaster VHF Ch 14.

Peterhead to Fraserburgh

Scotstown Head, 3½M north of Peterhead, is identified by a radio mast 107m in height. Drying and submerged reefs extend ½M off shore.

Between Scotstown Head and Rattray Head the installations of St Fergus Gas Terminal are conspicuous.

A lighthouse 34m in height stands on a rock off Rattray Head.

On Mormond Hill, 7M west of the point, military hardware and a TV mast are conspicuous.

Rattray Briggs with a depth of 0·3m lies nearly ½M east of the lighthouse, and shoals with a depth of little more than 2m extend 1M ESE from it.

Severe overfalls occur off Rattray Head, inevitably when the wind is against the tide.

When rounding Rattray Head careful note should be made of tidal streams and a good offing maintained.

At Cairnbulg Point, 6M NW of Rattray Head, a drying rock ledge extends 3 cables north, with a light beacon near its outer end.

Tides

At a point 5M NE of Rattray Head
The NW-going stream begins about +0140 Aberdeen (+0500 Dover)
The SE-going stream begins about –0440 Aberdeen (–0220 Dover).
Even at this distance from the shore the spring rate is up to 2 knots.

Fraserburgh

57°41'·5N 02°00'W

Charts

BA *1462* (1:20,000), *213* (1:75,000); Imray *C23* (1:250,000); OS Landranger *30*

Tides

Constant –0000 Aberdeen (+0338 Dover)
Heights in metres

MHWS	MHWN	MTL	MLWN	MLWS
3·5	2·8	2·2	1·6	0·7

Dangers and marks

Cairnbulg Briggs, a reef extending 3 cables from Cairnbulg Point, standing 2M ESE from Fraserburgh harbour entrance, is marked by a light beacon.

Kinnaird Head, close north of Fraserburgh, is marked by a white tower.

Fraserburgh Harbour is enclosed by breakwaters the heads of which are marked by light beacons.

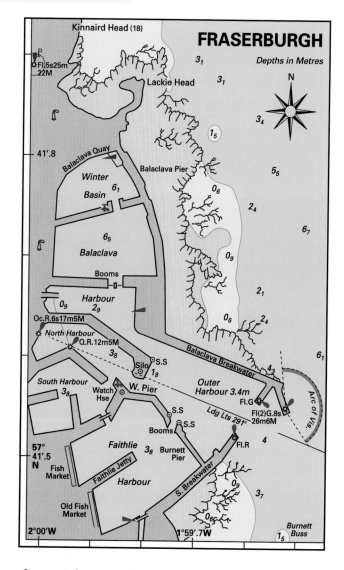

Approach

Call harbour on Ch 12 before entering.

Lights

Cairnbulg Briggs Fl(2)10s9m6M
Balaclava (north) breakwater head Fl(2)G.8s26m6M
South breakwater head Fl.R.6s4m5M
North breakwater spur Fl.G.6s3m5M
Ldg Lts 291° *Front* Q.R.12m5M *Rear* Oc.R.6s17m5M
Kinnaird Head Fl.5s25m22M

Supplies

Water and diesel, petrol at garage. *Calor Gas*, shops, PO, telephone, hotel. All repairs.

Harbourmaster VHF Ch 12 or ☎ 01346 515858. Office at South Harbour (watch tower on south side of outer harbour).

Fraserburgh

VI. Kinnaird Head to Lossiemouth

The passage along the coast is straightforward; with plenty of harbours, although some of them are unapproachable in certain wind directions and many are only accessible at certain states of tide. Suitable alternatives may be some distance apart. The length of this section is 41M.

Charts

BA *115* (1:200,000), *222, 223* (1:75,000); Imray *C23* (1:250,000); OS Landranger *27-30*
As an aid to exploring inshore, the OS Explorer (1:25,000) maps may be found helpful in this area – there are no Admiralty charts at this scale. Nos. *424-427* cover the coast from Fraserburgh to Lossiemouth.

Tides

The flood stream sets southward from Orkney, dividing off Spey Bay so that one branch runs in towards Inverness and the other towards Kinnaird Head.

Dangers and marks

The eastern part of the coast is low-lying.
Troup Head 110m high stands 9M W of Kinnaird Head.
Radio Mast on Windyheads Hill 3M SE of Troup Head.
Stotfield Head and Lossiemouth stand at the west side of Spey Bay, some 30M west of Troup Head.
Covesea Skerries lighthouse stands on the shore 2M west of Lossiemouth. Halliman Skerries, which dry 0·6m lie up to 6 cables off shore 1M NE of the lighthouse, marked by an unlit beacon, and Covesea Skerries, NW of the lighthouse, dry 1·8m.
Tarbat Ness lighthouse on the NW side of the Moray Firth is a white tower 41m in height with red bands.

Approaching the Moray Firth from seaward
Beatrice Oil Field lies 11M off the NW shore.
No.3 Y spar light buoy lies 15M off the S shore in approx. 2°50'W.

Lights
Kinnaird Head LtHo Fl.15s25m22M
Covesea Skerries LtHo Fl.WR.20s49m24/20M
Tarbat Ness Fl(4)30s53m24M

Harbours on the south side of the Moray Firth

The entrances to many harbours are narrow and sometimes tortuous. Keep a good lookout for fishing boats coming out, as they may be hidden behind a high screen wall.

Aberdeenshire and Banff and Buchan Councils provide a weekly 'season ticket' for a modest price to use any of the harbours owned and operated by those councils without restriction during a period of a week. Not all the harbours in this chapter are council owned, and in addition Johnshaven, Gourdon and Stonehaven in the previous chapter are owned by Aberdeenshire Council, and Hopeman and Burghead in the following chapter by Moray and Banff Council.

A free Directory of these harbours is available, including plans and tide tables; see Appendix I.

All harbours from Macduff westward have an hourly bus service between Aberdeen and Elgin, and thence to Inverness.

Sandhaven
⊕ ¼M north of entrance 57°42'·1N 02°03'·3W

The harbour, two miles west of Kinnaird Head, was decommissioned in 1935, and part of the breakwater has collapsed. It is expected that the harbour will be recommissioned in 2003, but the inner harbour dries, as does most of the outer harbour.

The bottom is sand over rock and visiting yachts which can dry out alongside the quay may enter at their own risk. There are no lights or leading marks at present but, particularly if heading east, this might be an attractive alternative to Fraserburgh.

Distances
Fraserburgh 2M, Rosehearty 2M.

Approach
After half flood with the head of the east breakwater bearing 180°, and only if no sea is running.
Secretary of the harbour users' committee
☎ 01346 511016.

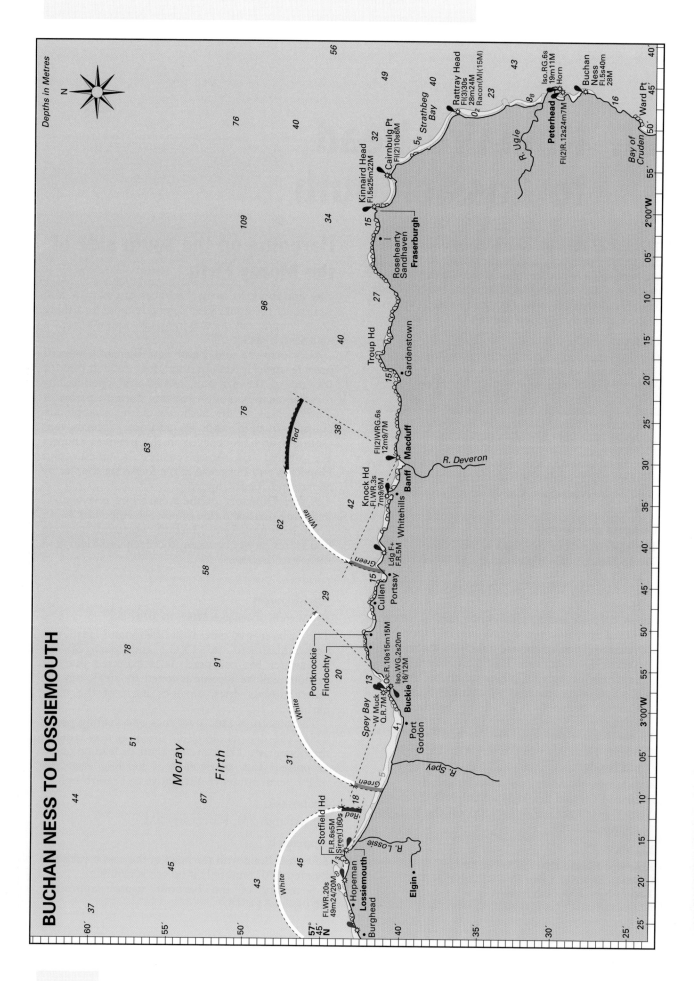

BUCHAN NESS TO LOSSIEMOUTH

Depths in Metres

N

Moray

Firth

56

76

40

109

96

76

63

58

29

62

42

34

15

Kinnaird Head
Fl.5s25m22M

32 Cairnbulg Pt
Fl(2)10s6M

56 Strathbeg
Bay

49

40 Rattray Head
Fl(3)30s
28m24M
0₂ Racon(M)(15M)

23

43

Iso.RG.6s
19m11M
Horn

Peterhead
Fl(2)R.12s24m7M

8₈

Buchan
Ness
Fl.5s40m
28M

16

Bay of
Cruden

50 Ward Pt

45

Rosehearty
Sandhaven
Fraserburgh

27

R. Ugie

Troup Hd

40

15

Gardenstown

R. Deveron

Red

38

White

Green

15

Knock Hd
Fl.WR.3s
7m9/6M

Fl(2)WRG.6s
12m9/7M

Macduff
Banff

Whitehills

Portsoy
Ldg F.+
F.R.5M

Cullen

78

91

51

31

White

Green

Portknockie

Findochty

20

13

Spey Bay

W. Muck
Q.R.7M

Oc.R.10s15m15M

Iso.WG.2s20m

Buckie 16/12M

41

Port
Gordon

R. Spey

White

45

45

43

Stotfield Hd

Red

18

Green

5

R. Lossie

Fl.R.6s5M
Siren(1)60s

Fl.WR.20s
49m24/20M

Hopeman

Lossiemouth

Burghead

Elgin

57°
45'
N

37

44

67

3°00'W

05'

60'

55'

50'

45'

40'

35'

30'

25'

2°00'W

05'

10'

15'

20'

25'

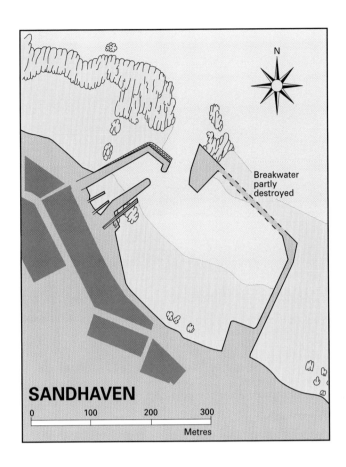

Rosehearty

⊕ ¼M 035°from breakwater head 57°42'·2N 02°06'·5W

A drying harbour, the entrance to which is protected from the west by a breakwater, which has a depth of 0·9m alongside, and on the head of which stands a stone beacon.

Distances

Fraserburgh 4M, Gardenstown 8M.

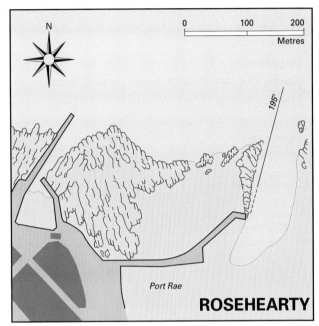

Rosehearty with Port Rae on left

Tides

Constant −0100 Aberdeen (+0218 Dover)

Approach

Parallel to the east face of the breakwater with a pair of black and white poles at the head of the harbour in line bearing approx. 215°. When 30m from the pier head keep mid way between the pier and the line of the poles. Avoid in onshore winds.

Port Rae, a drying area adjoining Rosehearty ¼M to the east, is sheltered from northwest by an extensive stone breakwater, but unmarked rocks lie inshore of it.

Supplies

Shops, PO, hotel, *Calor Gas* at caravan site.

Harbourmaster (home) ☎ 01346 571292.

Pennan

⊕ ½M north of harbour entrance 57°41'·3N 02°15'·5W

A tiny drying harbour with a photogenic village at the foot of cliffs, whose main claim to fame is as the location for part of the film *Local Hero*.

Dangers and marks

Howdman, a rock drying 2·9m lies 4 cables NNW of the harbour with shoal and drying rocks inshore, and Tamhead, drying 2·1m lies 3 cables NNE of the harbour.

Pennan

A radio mast on Windyhills, 2M inland, is conspicuous.

The harbour lies at the east end of the village.

Approach

After half flood and only if there is no swell, with the radio mast bearing 165°.

Pennan

Gardenstown

⊕ ¼M NNE of Craig Degarty 57°40'·8N 02°20'·2W

A drying harbour used by local pleasure boats and small inshore fishing boats, about two miles SW of Troup Head.

Distances

Macduff 6M, Rosehearty 8M.

Dangers and marks

Hill of Findon, ¾M south of the village is 194m high.

Craig Degarty, 4m high, stands on a drying reef 2 cables NNW of the harbour.

Powie Bushes, a rock drying 0·8m, lies 2 cables east of Craig Degarty.

The harbour dries with a bottom of hard sand.

Approach

Only if there is no swell, after half flood. Pass 1 cable east of Craig Degarty, steering 180° for the harbour entrance.

Harbour secretary ☎ 01261 851323.

Macduff

⊕ ½M NNW of entrance 57°40'·8N 02°30'·5W

A fishing harbour with some cargo traffic, with little space for yachts especially at weekends, although the fishing fleet is being depleted so rapidly that this may no longer apply. The entrance is only 10m wide, tortuous and exposed to NW, but reasonably sheltered from NE.

Charts

BA *1462* (1:20,000) (plan); Imray *C23* (plan); OS Landranger *29;* OS Explorer *426*

Distances

Fraserburgh 17M, Buckie 16M.

Tides

Constant −0120 Aberdeen (+0218 Dover)

Heights in metres

MHWS	MHWN	MTL	MLWN	MLWS
3·5	2·8	2·0	1·1	0·4

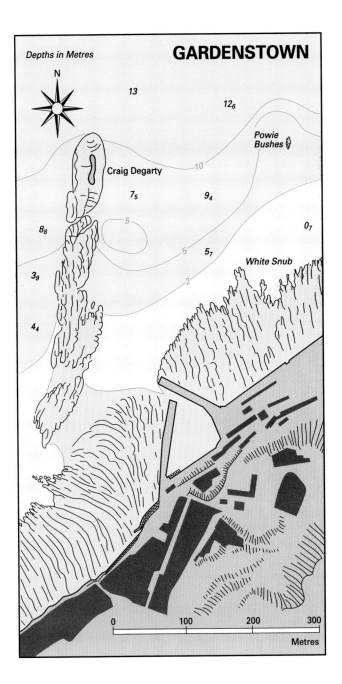

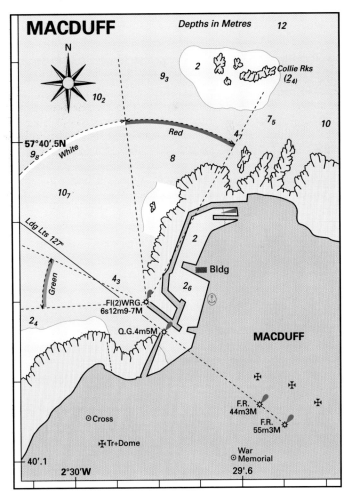

Gardenstown

Macduff

Dangers and marks

Collie Rocks, a detached reef drying 1·7m, lie up to ¼M NE of the harbour.

Submerged and drying reefs extend 1½ cables from the shore south of the entrance.

Approach

If from east keep at least 3 cables offshore and approach the entrance from NW. Look out for vessels leaving harbour.

Lights

NE pier head Fl(2)WRG.6s12m9-7M
West pier head Q.G.4m5M
Ldg Lts 127° *Front* F.R.44m3M *Rear* F.R.55m3M

At night

The white sector of the pier head light leads clear of off-lying dangers and the leading lights lead to the very narrow entrance.

Supplies

Water, petrol and diesel. *Calor Gas.* Shops, PO, telephone, bank. Open-air swimming pool. Boatyard, chandlery.

Harbourmaster VHF Ch 12 or ☎ 01261 832236. Office at east side of outer basin.

Banff

57°40'·2N 02°31'·W (⊕ as Macduff)

The harbour dries, and some dredging has been carried out and some cruising yachts are permanently moored there. Although many of the resident yachts have moved to Whitehills, a visiting yacht is unlikely to be able to lie afloat at LW.

Charts

Plan on BA *1462* (1:20,000); Imray *C23* (plan); OS Landranger *29*

Tides

Constant –0125 Aberdeen (+0055 Dover)
Heights in metres

MHWS	MHWN	MTL	MLWN	MLWS
3·5	2·8	2·0	1·1	0·4

Dangers and marks

Shoal and drying reefs lie up to 2 cables north and NE of the north breakwater, on the head of which stands a stone beacon, and drying reefs extend 1½ cables from the shore south of the entrance.

Do not approach in strong winds from between north and east, but in easterly winds Macduff is sheltered.

Lights

N pier head Fl.4s
Ldg Lts 295° *Front* Fl.R.4s *Rear* Q.R

Supplies

Water (and mains electricity) at the stone jetties inside the harbour; petrol and diesel at garages.

Banff

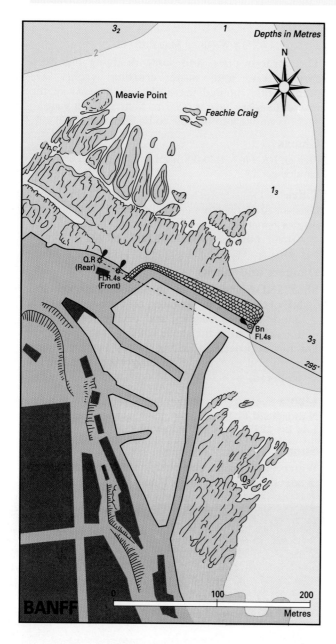

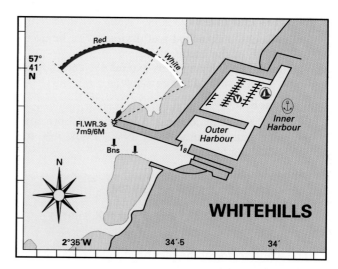

Calor Gas at caravan site, shops and supermarkets, PO, telephone, hotels, bank. Slipway and tidal grid. Showers at sailing club.

Harbourmaster ☎ 01261 815544.

Whitehills

⊕ ½M north of entrance 57°41'·5N 02°35'W

A clean, totally sheltered harbour with a depth of 1·1m throughout.

Distances

Macduff 3M, Portsoy 4M.

Tides

Constant –0135 Aberdeen (+0050 Dover)
Heights in metres

MHWS	MHWN	MTL	MLWN	MLWS
3·9	3·1	2·3	1·7	0·7

Dangers and marks

Drying reefs on the SW side of entrance channel are marked by beacons with triangular topmarks, of a rusty appearance so that they might be mistaken for port-hand beacons.

Approach

From NW between breakwater and beacons and turn sharp to port through very narrow opening. Look out for vessels coming out.

It may be possible to leave a yacht here for a few nights if necessary to break a passage.

50 pontoon berths are provided in the inner basin, two of which, on the outer ends are reserved for visitors.

Lights

Pier head Fl.WR.3s7m9/6M 132°-R-212°approach in red sector

Supplies

Water at the former fish market; the harbourmaster will supply a hose. Diesel may be available by tanker. *Calor Gas* at nearby caravan site. Shops, PO, telephone, bank in village.

Harbourmaster VHF Ch 08, 09 or ☎ 01261 861291

Portsoy

⊕ on leading line 3 cables NNW of entrance 57°41'·5N 02°41'·5W

A picturesque and ancient harbour which dries, but a yacht might lie afloat in the entrance to wait for the tide. Some inshore fishing boats and pleasure boats are berthed in the New Harbour which is completely sheltered but mostly dries, and a yacht which can take the ground may find space there.

Drying reefs extend up to a cable north of the harbour, to the east of the entrance.

Distances

Whitehills 4M, Cullen 4M.

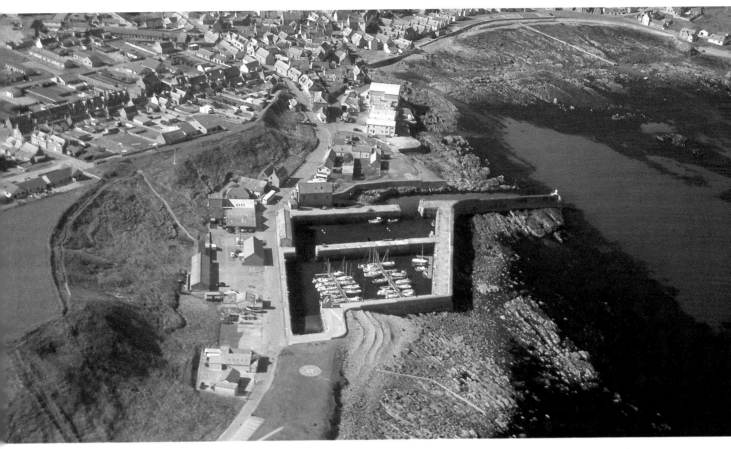

Whitehills   *(Photo: Former Grampian Regional Council)*

Portsoy   *(Photo: Former Grampian Regional Council)*

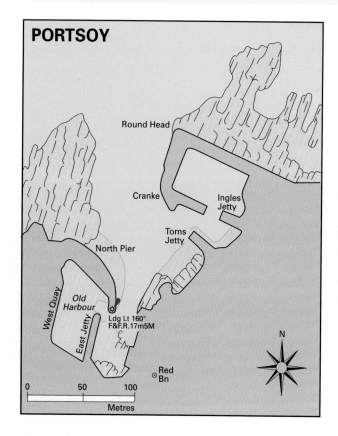

PORTSOY

Round Head

Cranke

Ingles Jetty

Toms Jetty

North Pier

West Quay

Old Harbour

East Jetty

Ldg Lt 160°
F&F.R.17m5M

Red Bn

0   50   100

Metres

N

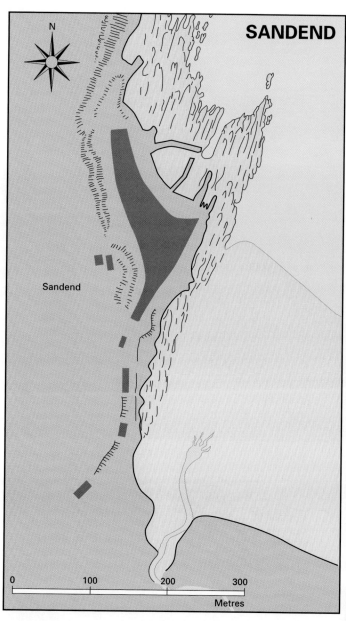

SANDEND

N

Sandend

0   100   200   300

Metres

Supplies

Petrol and diesel at garage. *Calor Gas* at caravan site, shops, PO, telephone, bank. Slipway.

Harbourmaster (at Banff) ☎ 01261 815544.

Sandend

57°41'N 02°45'W

A small privately-owned boat harbour, the features of which are shown in the photo.

Cullen

⊕ NW of entrance 57°41'·75 N 02°49'·60W

A small drying harbour used by inshore fishing boats, accessible above half tide to 1·5m draught, but only if there is no sea running.

The arches of a conspicuous disused railway viaduct identify the harbour.

Charts

OS Explorer *425*

Distances

Portsoy 4M, Portknockie 2M.

At night

A fixed green light is shown at the head of the outer basin.

Drying reefs extend up to a cable north of the harbour, on the east side of the entrance.

Sandend

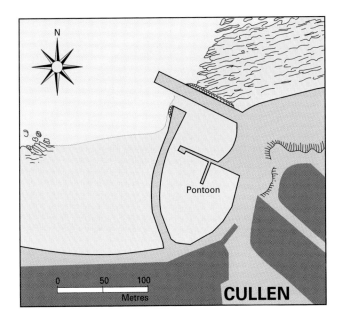

Cullen   *(Photo: Former Grampian Regional Council)*

Capel rock, which dries 0·2m, lies ½M NE of the entrance.

Supplies

Petrol and diesel at garage. *Calor Gas* at caravan site, shops, PO, telephone, hotel, bank.
Harbourmaster ☎ 01261 842477.

Portknockie
⊕ 57°42'·5N 02°52'W

Distances

Cullen 2M, Findochty 2M.

Tides

Constant –0135 Aberdeen (+0200 Dover).

Dangers and marks

Reefs extend a cable north of the harbour as well as more than a cable off shore in the bay west of the harbour entrance.

Lights

Fixed white leading lights bearing 143° lead to the entrance

Supplies

Water and electricity at harbour office, petrol and diesel at garage. *Calor Gas* at caravan site, shops, PO, telephone, bank.
Harbourmaster ☎ 01542 840833 (home). Office at S side of harbour.

Findochty
⊕ NW of entrance 57°42'·8N 02°54'·4W

Distances

Portknockie 2M, Buckie 3M.

Tides

Constant –0135 Aberdeen (+0043 Dover)

Dangers and marks

Drying reefs extend up to a cable north of the harbour, on the east side of the entrance, and rocks above water and drying lie on the west side of the entrance.
Beacon Rock stands ¾ cable NNW of the harbour entrance.

Portknockie

Findochty

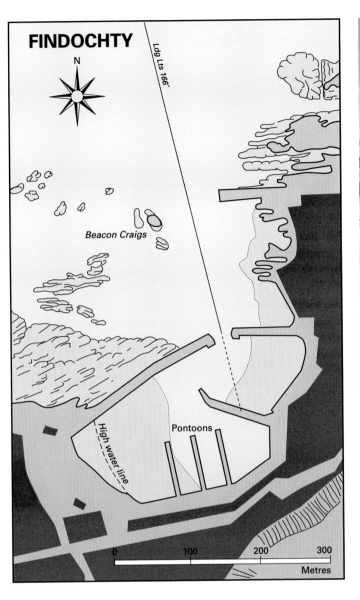

FINDOCHTY

N

Ldg Lts 166°

Beacon Craigs

High water line

Pontoons

0   100   200   300

Metres

Findochty

A sandbar, draught 0·2m obstructs the entrance to the outer harbour.

Approach

Above half tide only if there is no onshore sea, when it should be avoided.

Berth at pontoons in the west harbour, which mostly dries except at the middle pier and at the most easterly pontoons.

Lights

Ldg Lts 166° *Front* F.6m3M *Rear* F.10m3M

Supplies

Water and mains electricity at root of pontoons, petrol and diesel at garage. *Calor Gas* at caravan site, shop, PO, telephone, bank.

Harbourmaster ☎ 01542 831466. Office at east side of harbour.

Buckie

⊕ 1½ cables west of West Muck beacon, on line of leading lights, 57°41'·32N 02°58'·2W

A busy fishing harbour with some cargo traffic, but with space for yachts in the innermost basin. The entrance is 18m wide, and exposed to the NW. Look out for vessels coming out of the harbour.

Distances

Macduff 15M, Lossiemouth 11M.

Charts

BA *1462* (1:10,000) (plan); Imray *C23* (plan); OS Landranger *28*

Tides

Constant −0135 Aberdeen (+0040 Dover)

Heights in metres

MHWS	MHWN	MTL	MLWN	MLWS
4·1	3·2	2·4	1·6	0·7

Dangers and marks

Three groups of rocks, East, Middle, and West Muck, lie north and NE of the entrance with clear water inshore of them. A tripod light beacon stands on West Muck.

Approach

From east Note East Muck dries 2·9m and keep ½M off shore.

Pass at least ½ cable west of West Muck heading for the harbour entrance. Look out for vessels coming out.

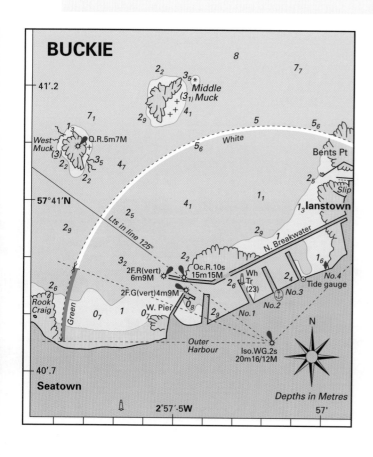

BUCKIE

8

7_7

2_2 3_{5} ✳

41'.2

Middle Muck
(3) 1_1

7_1

2_9 4_1

5

5_6

West Muck (3)

1_3 Q.R.5m7M

White

5_6

Bents Pt

2_2 3_5

4_7

2_5

57°41'N

2_5

4_1

1_1

1_3 **Ianstown**

Slip

2_9

2_9

2_9 N. Breakwater

Lts in line 125°

3_2

2_2

1_6

2F.R(vert) 6m9M

Oc.R.10s 15m15M

Wh Tr (23)

2_4 No.4 Tide gauge

2_6

2_6

$2F.G(vert)4m9M

No.3

2_6

Rook Craig

0_7

1

0_7

W. Pier

0_8

No.2

2_9

No.1

Green

N

Outer Harbour

Iso.WG.2s 20m16/12M

40'.7

Seatown

2°57'·5W

57'

Depths in Metres

Call HM on VHF before approaching. Yachts usually berth in No.4 basin.

Lights

Ldg mark *Front* Oc.R.10s15m15M
Rear Iso.WG.2s20m16/12M
West Muck Q.R.5m7M
NW pier head 2F.R(vert)9M
S side entrance 2F.G(vert)9M

At night

The light on West Muck together with the leading lights make the approach straightforward. Note the leading lights do not lead to the entrance, but clear west of West Muck.

Shelter

Complete once inside but entrance may be hazardous for a low-powered yacht in onshore winds.

Services and supplies

Water on quays, petrol from garages, diesel by tanker. Shop, PO, telephone. Boatyard.

Harbourmaster VHF Ch 12 (24 hours) or ☎ 01542 831700.

Buckie

Portgordon

57°40'N 03°01'W

A small drying harbour owned by the Crown Estate, used by a few small inshore fishing boats.

Craigan Roan, a rock drying 2·3m, lies 1 cable NNW of the harbour.

Mouth of the Spey, Kingston, Garmouth

Sea-going ships used to be built here with timber floated down the river, but the river mouth is now inaccessible except to shoal-draught boats and then only in millpond conditions.

Portgordon

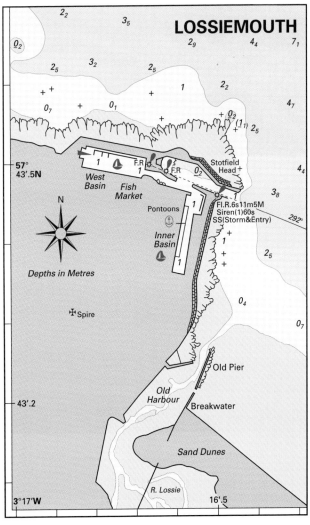

Lossiemouth

57°43'·4N 03°16'·4W

A former fishing harbour now equipped with yacht pontoons in both basins. The entrance is shallow and may be closed in easterly gales.

Distances

Buckie 11M, Burghead 8M.

Charts

BA *1462* (1:6,250) (plan); OS Landranger *28*

Lossiemouth

Covesea and Halliman Skerries

Tides

Constant –0140 Aberdeen (+0040 Dover)
Heights in metres

MHWS	MHWN	MTL	MLWN	MLWS
4·1	3·2	2·4	1·6	0·6

Dangers and marks

Halliman Skerries ¾M off shore with a beacon 15m high on the highest point, lie 1½M west of Stotfield Head.

Drying reefs and submerged rocks lie more than a cable north of Stotfield Head.

Approach

From west give Halliman Skerries a wide berth.

Look out for vessels coming out from the harbour.

Lights

S pier Fl.R.6s11m5M
Ldg Lts 292° F.R

Shelter

Complete once inside, but entrance may be hazardous for a low-powered yacht in onshore winds.

Supplies

Water, petrol and diesel. *Calor Gas*, shops, PO, telephone.

Marine Engineers: Henry Fleetwood and Sons ☎ 01343 813015. Showers, launderette.

Harbourmaster VHF Ch 12 (office hours) or ☎ 01343 813066.

VII. Inner Moray Firth and Caledonian Canal

Stotfield Head to Chanonry Point

The distance from Stotfield Head to Chanonry Point at the entrance to Inverness Firth is 30M and to Tarbat Ness, on the north shore of the Moray Firth, is about 18M. From Chanonry Point to the entrance to the Caledonian Canal is 7M.

Charts

BA *223* (1:75,000), *1077* (1:20,000); Imray *C23* (1:250,000); OS Explorer *422, 423*

Tides

The flood stream sets into the Moray Firth.

Dangers and marks

Halliman and Covesea Skerries extend ¾M offshore west of Stotfield Head, on which Lossiemouth stands. A beacon marks the east end of the skerries.

Covesea Skerries lighthouse is a conspic. white tower on the shore.

Tarbat Ness lighthouse on the NW side of the Moray Firth is a white tower 41m in height with red bands.

Three Kings reef, 10M SW of Tarbat Ness, is marked on its east side by an east cardinal light buoy.

Fairway RWVS light buoy lies in the middle of the inner Moray Firth about 3M ESE of the entrance to the Cromarty Firth.

Riff Bank, which partly dries, south of the approach to the Narrows at Fort George, is marked by light buoys.

McDermott Base, on the south shore has large conspicuous sheds and sometimes an oil production platform under construction.

North channel is marked as follows; each buoy is well clear of any hazard to a yacht, but there is no satisfactory mark for the most dangerous part of Riff Bank, which rises from 7m to drying in less than a cable.

Riff Bank East light buoy, Y spherical
Riff Bank North light buoy, R can
Riff Bank West light buoy, Y spherical

Navity Bank starboard-hand light buoy north of Riff Bank marks the southern extremity of a bank on which the least depth is 2·3m.

Drying banks and shoal water extend up to 3 cables off the NW shore to west of *Navity Bank* buoy.

Craigmee light buoy, NW of Fort George, marks a shoal bank north of the east point of Chanonry narrows.

Buckle Rock, with less than 2m, lies 4 cables from the west shore WNW of *Craigmee* buoy.

Chanonry Point lighthouse, white, 13m in height, Oc.6s12m15M stands at the SE end of Chanonry Ness, at the west side of the narrows.

South channel is marked as follows:
Riff Bank South light buoy.

A small red can buoy ¼M further south, at the entrance to the channel to McDermott Base, and a green conical buoy a cable southwest of it, lie near the north end of White Ness Sand which dries up to ¾M from the south shore. This bank is very steep-to and otherwise unmarked.

White Ness Sand extends up to ¾M from the south shore west of McDermott Base, separated from Riff Bank by the poorly-marked South Channel.

Lights

Covesea Skerries LtHo Fl.WR.20s49m24/20M
Tarbat Ness LtHo Fl(4)30s53m24M
Three Kings Lt buoy Q(3)10s
Fairway Lt buoy LFl.10s
Riff Bank East Lt buoy Fl.Y.10s
Navity Bank Lt buoy Fl(3)G.15s
Riff Bank North Lt buoy Fl(2)R.12s
Riff Bank South Lt buoy Q(6)+LFl.15s
Riff Bank West Lt buoy Fl.Y.5s
Craigmee Lt buoy Fl.R.6s
Chanonry Point LtHo Oc.6s12m15M

Hopeman

57°43'N 03°26'W

Charts

BA *1462* (1:6250) (plan); Imray *C23* (plan); OS Landranger *28*

Distances

Lossiemouth 5M, Burghead 3M

Tides

Constant −0140 Aberdeen (+0050 Dover)

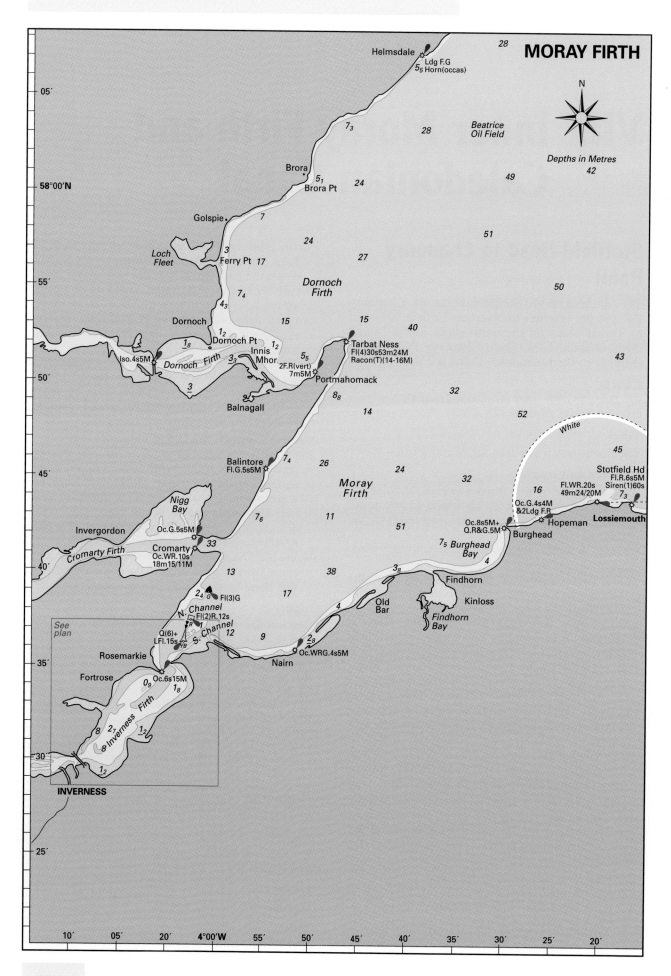

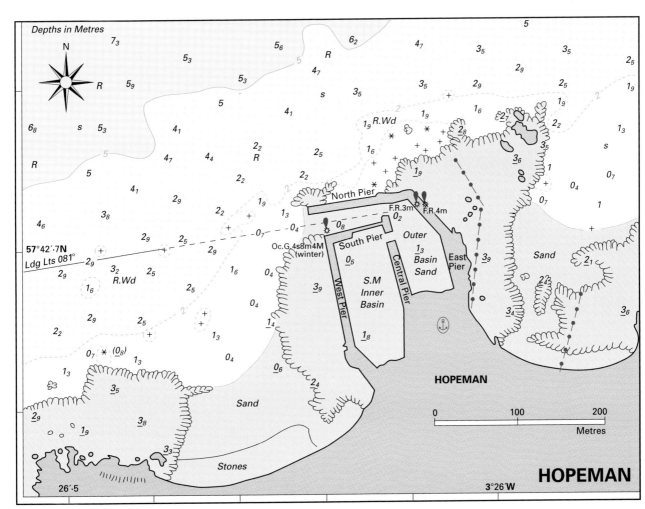

Hopeman

Dangers and marks

Submerged rocks lie about 75m west of the entrance. Approach from north keeping about 25m off the end of the outer pier.

Lights

West pier Oc.G.4s8m4M
Ldg Lts 081° F.R

Supplies

Water, diesel Gas, shops, PO, telephone.

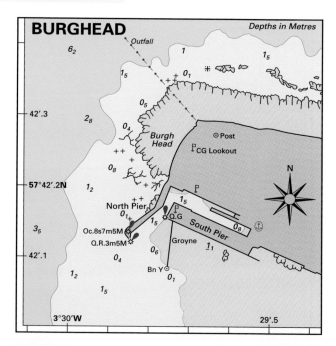

Burghead

57°42'N 03°30'W

A small harbour in which are based many fishing boats, so that there may be no space for yachts, although proposals are being considered for developing a marina.

This is one of the few harbours which may be safely entered in easterly winds. Approach from northwest and keep to the port side of the channel

Burghead   *(Photo: Former Grampian Regional Council)*

where the water is deepest. Yachts drawing 1·5m should be able to enter at LWS.

In strong NW winds Lossiemouth may be a better option.

Distances

Lossiemouth 8M, Findhorn 7M.

Charts

BA *1462* (1:6,250) (plan); Imray *C23* (plan); OS Landranger *28*

Tides

Constant –0120 Aberdeen (+0218 Dover)

Heights in metres

MHWS	MHWN	MTL	MLWN	MLWS
4·1	3·2	2·4	1·6	0·6

Dangers and marks

Drying rocks extend offshore north and northwest of the entrance.

Lights

N breakwater Oc.8s7m5M
B breakwater, S end Q.R.3m5M
South pier head Q.G.3m5M

Supplies

Water, diesel. *Calor Gas*, petrol, shops, PO, telephone, chandlery.

Harbourmaster's office at north quay, VHF Ch 12.

Findhorn

⊕ RW Pillar Buoy 57°40'·33N 03°38'·94W

The entrance to the bay is obstructed by drying banks whose positions change frequently in a manner which will be familiar to those who sail from the Ore or the Deben in Suffolk, or among the Frisian Islands.

Boats drawing 1·5 metres can enter at half tide in quiet weather.

A drying bank extends westward from the spit at the east side of the entrance and the channel normally lies on a north-south orientation, marked by port-hand light buoy.

The tidal stream runs strongly in the entrance as the bay fills and empties.

Fairway RWVS pillar buoy lies off the bar.

Distances

Burghead 7M, Nairn 9M, Cromarty 14M.

Tides

Constant –0140 Aberdeen (+0200 Dover)

Heights in metres

MHWS	MHWN	MTL	MLWN	MLWS
4·1	3·2	2·4	1·6	0·6

Dangers and marks

A windsock stands on the point east of the entrance and a wind generator about a mile inland, further east.

A port-hand light buoy marks the Bar, followed by two starboard-hand light buoys. Keep three boat lengths from the perches on the beach.

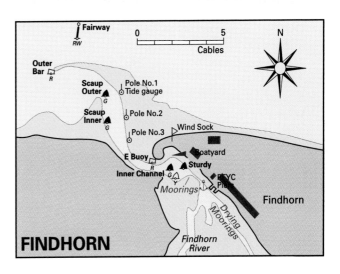

The Scaup is a hard ridge extending north from the shore south of the entrance channel.

Three pile beacons stand on the east side of the channel, which is steep-to at this point.

Approach

Coming from east keep outwith the 3-metre contour until the pillar buoy is identified. Look for vessels coming out.

On the most northerly of three poles mark the edge of the drying sands at the east side of the channel is a tide gauge which should be visible through binoculars from the *Landfall* buoy. If any of the red section shows there is less than 2m in the channel, and at the top of the white section there is 3m. If there is too little water to enter the holding is good off the entrance, with a sandy bottom.

Turn to port when past the bar buoy, and identify *Scaup Outer* buoy, which will appear to starboard of the windsock at this point, keeping a close watch on the echo sounder.

The depth increases after passing the bar buoy, but the shallowest part of the channel lies north of *Scaup Outer* buoy. The three poles should be left three boat lengths to port heading south, and all buoys passed a boat length off.

Pass east of *Scaup Inner* buoy, opposite the middle pole, and follow the channel round to port to pass south of a port-hand buoy south of the three poles, then north and east of two starboard-hand buoys, *Inner Channel* and *Sturdy*.

Anchor clear of moorings wherever enough depth is found, either off the boatyard or to the south of the stone piers. Visitors moorings are available.

The Royal Findhorn Yacht Club is very hospitable to visitors, A phone call to the RFYC or the boatyard in advance would be prudent. A VHF call when off the entrance may yield a response.

RFYC ☎ 01309 690247. Boatyard ☎ 01309 690099.

Supplies

Water and electricity at north stone pier, petrol and diesel from garage. *Calor Gas*, chandlery at boatyard, shops, pubs, restaurant in village, PO, telephone. Boatyard.

Findhorn

Findhorn

Old Bar

57°40'·3N 02°30'W

An inlet 2½M west of Findhorn which provides a completely sheltered anchorage to any yacht which succeeds in finding her way in. No stranger should attempt this without first seeking advice from either Royal Findhorn YC or Nairn SC.

The entrance varies from year to year, and it is normally marked by a white buoy provided by Nairn SC.

A survey was carried out in May 2002 by RA and MRA Fresson, when a waypoint at the entrance was established at 57°38'·878N 3°45'·29W (WGS 84 datum). The depth at this point was 0·25m at LWS, and increases steadily to 2·0m at the anchorage. From the entrance waypoint steer on a bearing of 107°, keeping the sandbank on the port side as close aboard as possible. The anchorage is WSW of the salmon bothy. There is usually a tide through the anchorage and anchored yachts will almost always lie to the tide so there is little or no swinging while at anchor outwith the direction of tidal stream. Yachts entering the Old Bar for the first time are advised to put a lookout on the bow or crosstrees as the dark course of the channel is quite visible to the eye on a bright day.

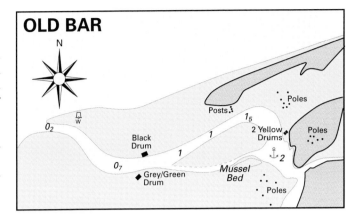

Nairn

57°35'·6N 03°51'·6W

An artificial harbour at a river mouth entered between breakwaters over a drying bar with pontoon berths in a dock on the starboard side of the entrance channel.

Distances

Burghead 14M, Fortrose 10M, Cromarty 14M.

Charts

BA *1462* (1:6,250) (plan); OS Landranger *27*

Tides

Constant –0120 Aberdeen (+0218 Dover)
Heights in metres

MHWS	MHWN	MTL	MLWN	MLWS
4·3	3·3	2·5	1·6	0·7

Old Bar entrance

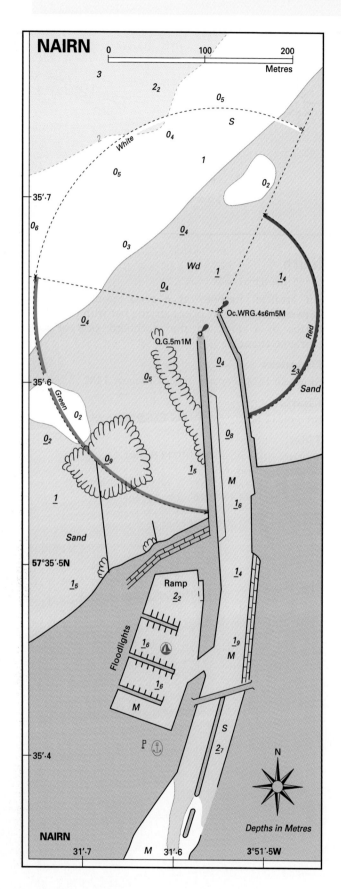

NAIRN

0   100   200

Metres

NAIRN

Depths in Metres

Dangers and marks

The channel outside the entrance dries completely. Light beacons on pier heads.

Approach

Within 2 hours of HW only.
Harbourmaster ☎ 01667 454704.
Nairn Sailing Club ☎ 01667 453897.

Harbours on north side of Moray Firth

Balintore

⊕ ¼M south of East pier head 57°45'N 03°54'·6W

Distances

Cromarty 7M, Findhorn 11M.

Dangers and marks

Three Kings reef, more than ½M from the shore, 1½M south of Balintore, is marked by an east

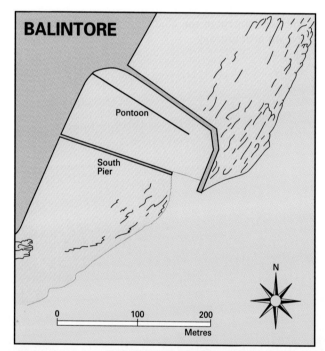

BALINTORE

Pontoon

South
Pier

N

0   100   200

Metres

Balintore

Nairn harbour entrance

Balintore

cardinal light buoy. Fixed salmon nets may be laid northeast of the harbour.

Approach

If from northward, keep ½M off shore to avoid salmon nets.

The bottom is hard sand, which should be kept in mind if staying long enough to take the ground and there is any onshore sea.

Lights

Three Kings light buoy Q(3)10s
E pier head Fl.G.5s5m5M

Supplies

Shop, PO, telephone, hotel.

Cromarty Firth

⊕ Fairway buoy 57°40'·0N 03°54'·0W

As far back as the 15th century the Cromarty Firth was noted by Alexander Lindsay, pilot to King James IV as 'above all havens in the yle of Britane for Saiftie of shippis both great and small is the Fyrth of Crumbertie for all kynd of windis and storme, in which haven schippis may enter at al tyme of flood'.

Although the firth as a whole is well sheltered there is a lack of harbours or mooring places for small craft, except the harbour of Cromarty itself, where a berth afloat may be found at the north side. Nigg Bay on the north shore within the entrance is occupied by oil industry works.

14M from the entrance the firth is crossed by a bridge with 3m headroom.

At times the firth is occupied by oil rigs, being repaired or refurbished, or dismantled, or abandoned.

Chart

BA *1889*, (*1890*) (1:15,000); OS Landranger *27*

Tides

The in-going stream begins about +0605 Aberdeen (−0400 Dover).
The out-going stream begins about −0105 Aberdeen (+0115 Dover).
Constant −0130 Aberdeen (+0100 Dover)

Heights in metres

MHWS	MHWN	MTL	MLWN	MLWS
4·3	3·4	2·6	1·7	0·8

Distances

From Cromarty: Findhorn 17M, Chanonry Point 9M.

Dangers and marks

A buoyed fairway leads from *Fairway* buoy through the entrance narrows. This fairway is used by large commercial vessels.

Lights

Fairway buoy LFl.10s
Cromarty Bank G con buoy Fl(2)G.10s
Buss Bank R can buoy Fl.R.3s
Cromarty LtHo Oc.WR.10s18m.15/11M
Nigg Terminal pier Oc.G.5s5M

Cromarty

⊕ 1 cable NW of harbour entrance 57°41'·1N 04°02'·4W

A small town on the south side of the entrance to the Firth.

Distances

Portmahomack 20M, Findhorn 14M

The harbour is subject to scend with winds between SW and NE.

Visiting yachts may be able to moor temporarily on the east side (inside) of the outer pier.

The outer part of the east pier is closed off from the landward side, and yachts should not make fast there.

Anchor southwest of pier, but not inshore of the continuation of line of the face of the pier head as the water shoals abruptly.

Tides

Constant −0130 Aberdeen (+0110 Dover)

Heights in metres

MHWS	MHWN	MTL	MLWN	MLWS
4·3	3·4	2·5	1·7	0·8

Anchorage

SW of outer pier.

Supplies

Shops, PO, telephone, hotel in town.

Cromarty is the birthplace of Hugh Miller, a pioneer of geology, and his cottage is maintained by the National Trust for Scotland.

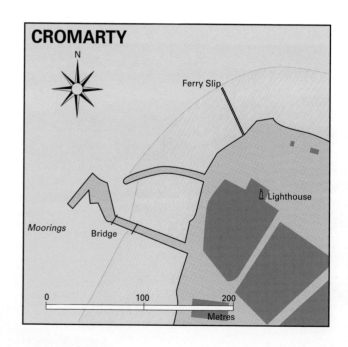

Invergordon

There is a boat harbour among the industrial installations on the north side of the firth, but the harbour authority makes little provision for small craft, although Invergordon Boat Club welcomes visitors (Hon. Sec. ☎ 01349 877612).

Inverness Firth

Charts

BA *1078* (1:20,000); Imray *C23* (plan); OS Explorer *432*

Chanonry Narrows

⊕ 3 cables west of Chanonry Point 57°34'·5N 04°05'W

Tides

At the Narrows

The SW-going stream begins about +0605 Aberdeen (–0400 Dover).

The NE-going stream begins about –0105 Aberdeen (+0115 Dover).

In each case there is 1¼ hours slack water before the tide turns. The spring rate off Fort George is 2½ knots.

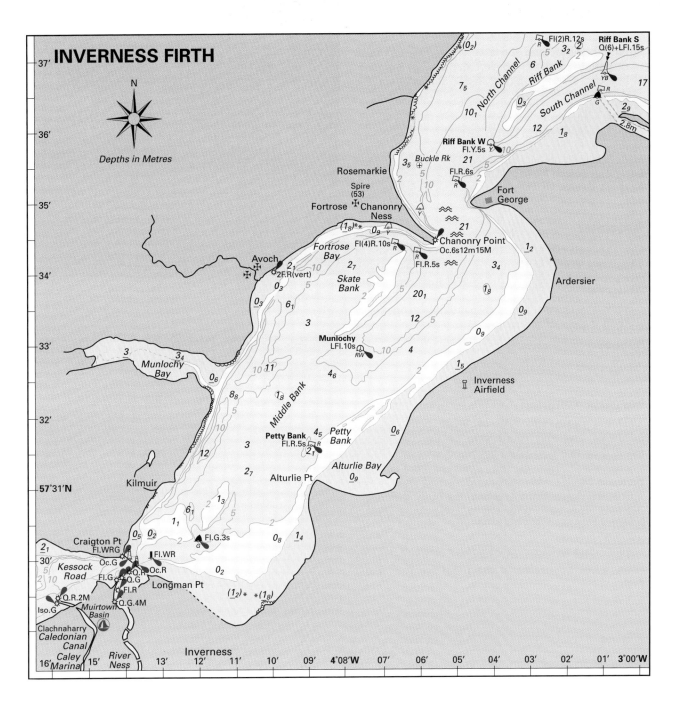

Dangers and marks

Within the Firth the main fairway lies on the SE side of Skate Bank, but drying foreshore and shoal water extends ½M off the SE shore of the firth, and up to a mile off Alturlie Bay, marked by a red can buoy lying about ¾M north of Alturlie Point.

Skate Bank lies NW of the middle of the firth; a possibly confusing port-hand light buoy SSW of Chanonry Point marks the NE corner of the bank and the beginning of Fortrose Channel, for which see below.

Munlochy RWVS light buoy lies in mid-channel east of the south end of the bank.

Kessock Bridge, across Kessock Narrows, lies 6M SW of Chanonry Point.

Middle Bank, a shoal extending from the west shore north of Kessock Bridge is marked by a starboard-hand light buoy SE of its east end. A detached shoal lies north of the buoy.

Drying foreshore and shoal water extends 1M from the south and SE shore, marked by *Longman* beacon, a red structure inside the edge of the drying bank.

Lights

Chanonry Point LtHo Oc.6s12m15M
Munlochy Lt buoy LFl.10s
Middle Bank Lt buoy Fl.G.3s4M
Longman beacon Fl.WR.2s7m5/4M
Kessock Bridge Oc.R.6s28m5M and Oc.G.6s28m5M

Ardersier

On the east shore of the firth, 1½M ESE of Chanonry Point lighthouse, a yellow beacon with cross topmark stands at the end of a sewer outfall, on the LW line.

A slipway lies inshore of the outfall beacon.

Anchor clear of moorings.

Supplies

Shops, hotel and fuel.

Fortrose Channel

This lies north and NW of Skate bank. At the northeast end the south side of the channel is marked by two port-hand light buoys.

The south end of the Fortrose channel lies between Meikle Mee and the detached shoal to its northeast. Apart from *Middle Bank* buoy which lies between the east point of Meikle Mee and a detached shoal, this end of the channel is not defined.

The tidal stream in Fortrose Channel runs counter to the stream in the main fairway of the firth.

Fortrose

⊕ in channel south of pier head 57°34'·5N 04°08'W

Dangers and marks

Craig an Roan, 2 cables east of the harbour, which dries 1·8m, is marked by a perch with a triangular topmark (may be missing).

Anchor off the pier, which dries, clear of moorings. Sailing club members are most helpful. In easterlies some shelter will be found under the lee of Chanonry Point.

Supplies

Shops, PO, telephone, hotel.

Fortrose

Avoch

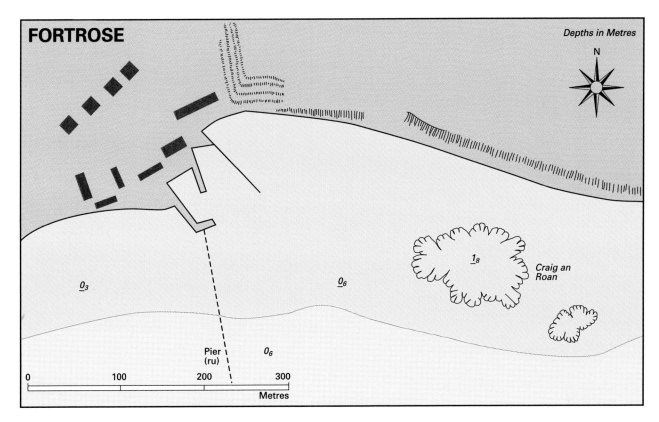

Avoch

57°34'N 04°10'W

The harbour dries, but may be entered at half tide.

Light

S pier head 2F.R(vert)7m5M(occas)

Supplies

Water, petrol and diesel at garage. Shops, PO, telephone, hotel.

Munlochy Bay

Munlochy Bay

57°32'·4N 04°11'·5W

Mostly dries, with a channel as shown in the photo, and there is no regular anchorage.

The channel enters the firth close to the south point of the bay, over a bar with a depth of 0·5m, and a pool ¼M within the entrance has a depth of 2·1m. Not recommended without local knowledge.

Kessock Narrows

⊕ mid channel, under bridge 57°30'N 04°13'·7W

Tides

The in-going stream begins about +0535 Aberdeen (−0430 Dover).

The out-going stream begins about −0150 Aberdeen (+0130 Dover).

The in-going stream runs at 4 knots, and the out-going, augmented by run-off from rivers, may reach 6 knots. There is ½ hour slack water before the tide turns at HW, and 2 hours at LW.

During and after heavy rain there is a sharply defined boundary between the current flowing out from the River Ness and the tide flooding through Kessock Narrows to the Beauly Firth).

An eddy runs along the north side of the narrows west of the bridge on the flood.

Constant −0120 Aberdeen (+0100 Dover)

Heights in metres

MHWS	MHWN	MTL	MLWN	MLWS
4·8	3·7	2·8	1·8	0·7

Kessock Bridge. Note tidal stream under bridge

Inverness Harbour

57°29'·55N 04°14'·1W

Dangers and marks

Drying banks on the south and east side of the approach to the harbour are marked by two red light-beacons standing at the low water line.

A drying spit on the west side of the river extends almost to the middle of the Firth. If proceeding from Inverness Harbour to the canal, yachts should retrace their steps to the outer port-hand beacon before turning west.

Approach

Pass north of *Outer* and *Inner* beacons, heading for Embankment Head; check constantly to see that you are not being set off course by the current.

Berth

At outermost pontoons or at quayside, and consult harbourmaster.

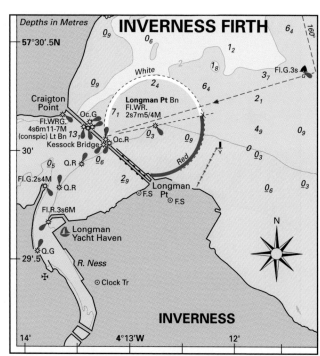

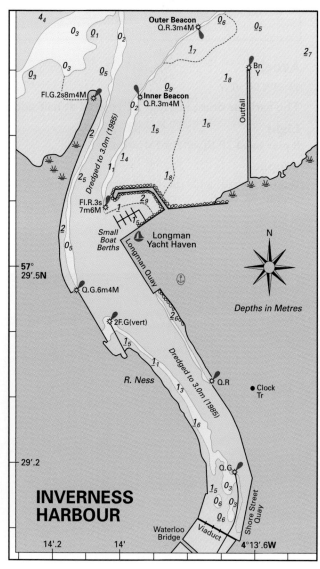

Lights

Craigton Point Bn (N shore) Fl.WRG.4s6m11-7M
Outer Bn Q.R.3m4M
Inner Bn Q.R.3m4M
Embankment head Fl.G.2s8m4M
Turning Bn (E side) Fl.R.3s7m6M
Thornbush Wharf Q.G.6m4M
Slipway 2F.G(vert)4m3M
Citadel quay Q.R.5m3M
Training Wall head Q.G.5m4M

Supplies

Water at yacht haven and alongside quays, petrol diesel and *Calor Gas* at quays. Mechanical and electrical engineers. Shops, PO, telephone, hotel in city. Chandlery (Gael Force Marine, at north side of harbour ☎ 01463 229400). Chart agent at Caley Marina, see below.

Harbourmaster VHF Ch 12 (office hours) ☎ 01463 715715. Office at N End of Citadel Quay.

Clachnaharry Lock

⊕ 1 cable NW of entrance 57°29'·5N 04°15'·9W

The entrance lock for the Caledonian Canal. Yachts may enter the canal even if not intending to pass through, but the charges for a short stay are particularly high.

The lock is entered between piled training walls extending WNW from the shore. There is often a strong current running out from the lock across the tidal stream running in the firth.

The lock is only opened within 4 hours of high water. For general opening times see Caledonian Canal, below.

Before the lock opens keep clear of the approach.

It is obviously preferable to approach with a rising tide. There is nowhere to wait except at anchor. The jetties at either side of the entrance are of open pile construction.

As an alternative to anchoring off the sea lock, it may be preferable to anchor at Fortrose or Ardersier at the mouth of the firth, or moor at the marina in Inverness Harbour.

In the canal after passing through the sea lock there are stagings for mooring.

Dangers

The drying foreshore extends outwith a straight line between the old ferry slip to the east and the ends of the training walls at the sea lock, and shoal water lies west of the west pier.

Approach

From Kessock Bridge keep north of mid-channel until one cable east of the old ferry slip at North Kessock before making for the sea lock to avoid shoal ground on the south side of the channel.

Lights

West pier Iso.G.4s5m2M
East pier Q.R.5m2M

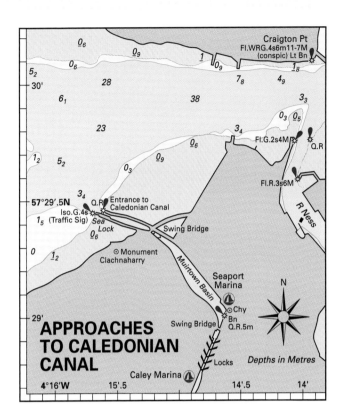

APPROACHES TO CALEDONIAN CANAL

Anchorage

2 cables NW of the entrance in a depth of 8–10m to avoid swinging into shallow water.

Supplies

Water at sea lock, shop, telephone at Clachnaharry, lock-keeper VHF Ch 74.

Beauly Firth extends 6M west of Kessock Bridge. Sandbanks encumber the firth, but they are unmarked and no current Admiralty chart covers it.

Caledonian Canal

The canal was built in the early 19th century to avoid the long and exposed passage round the north of Scotland. In fact, the distance from Fraserburgh to any place north of Mallaig is actually less by the coast, and the time taken may be much less in moderate weather. However the passage through the canal is extremely picturesque, and visitors to the West Coast often plan to go one way and return the other.

Short sections of man-made canal link three freshwater lochs, and in a total length of 52M only 18M are artificial cuts. The greatest height above sea level, at Loch Oich, is 32m and there are 29 locks, many of them grouped into 'staircases', in which the top gate of one lock is the bottom gate of the next.

The wind tends to funnel along the length of the lochs in a SW or NE direction, and seas in the fresh water are steeper than a wind of similar strength would raise in sea water.

Clachnaharry Sea Lock

Charts BA *1791* (1:75,000) (plans); OS Landranger (1:50.000) *26, 34, 41*; OS Explorer *392, 400, 416.*

Maximum dimensions 44·7m x 10·7m x 4·1m draught. All bridges open during working hours, but the frequency of opening may depend on road traffic.

The canal is open as follows: From mid-May to early October, seven days a week 0800–1800; from mid-March to mid-May, and October to beginning of November, Monday to Saturday 0800–1650; November to mid-March Monday to Friday 0915–1600.

There may be some variations on these times from year to year, and for the exact dates between which the times apply, check with the canal office.

During the winter there are often long closures for repairs and improvements.

A speed limit of 5 knots operates throughout the canal section. The whole passage takes a minimum of two days.

There are no restrictions on sailing on the lochs at night but the only navigation lights, at each end of Loch Ness and at the south end of Loch Lochy, are not shown in summer as the canal closes before dark.

Charter boats operate throughout the canal until mid-October.

Pontoons and stagings are heavily used by hire cruisers.

Throughout the canal and lochs the NW side of the channel is marked by red buoys and beacons, and the SE by green. A brief description of the canal from NE to SW follows:

A railway swing-bridge crosses the canal, ¼M inland from the sea lock, where there may be delays if a train is due to pass. Immediately south of the bridge is a lock leading into Muirtown Basin.

Seaport Marina lies on the northeast side of Muirtown Basin (for services, etc. see below).

A road bridge across the canal at the south end of Muirtown Basin may not be opened during morning and evening rush hours. Beyond the bridge is a staircase of four locks.

Yachts may moor at Seaport Marina, which has a security fence, or above Muirtown Locks, although security may be a problem there, or at Caley Marina, beyond Muirtown Locks (Caley Marina, together with Caley Cruisers, was founded by Jim

Hire cruisers milling about in Fort Augustus locks

Hogan, without whose initiative and subsequent diplomacy at moments of crisis the canal certainly would not have survived). Yachts in transit finding themselves in Muirtown Basin at closing time may moor at Seaport Marina without additional charge.

Charges are made for mooring at these and other commercial facilities, but mooring places at locks and wharves provided by British Waterways are generally free of charge.

Yachts will not normally be accepted within 1½ hours of LWS owing to lack of water over the lock sill. The time covered by a Passage Licence is currently increased to a week.

Services at Inverness

Both Seaport and Caley marinas provide water, diesel, electricity, mechanical and electrical repairs, crane, *Calor Gas*, showers. Caley Marina also sells chandlery and is an Admiralty Chart Agent. Seaport is a little closer to the city centre. Canal office ☎ 01463 233140. Sea Lock ☎ 01463 713896. Seaport Marina ☎ 01463 239475. Caley Marina ☎ 01463 236539.

There is likely to be a delay at main road bridges to gather together several boats, to avoid frequently holding up road traffic.

From the head of Muirtown Locks a section of canal, with one bridge, and Dochgarroch lock leads to Loch Dochfour, effectively an extension to Loch Ness. There are stagings at Dochgarroch Lock, and space to anchor in Loch Dochfour.

The distance from the top of Dochgarroch Lock, along Loch Ness to Fort Augustus is 21M.

Most of Loch Ness is too deep for anchoring, but on the NW shore it is possible to anchor in Urquhart Bay (57°20'N 04°27'W), north of the ruins of Urquhart Castle.

Urquhart Bay Marina provides berths for yachts on passage, and there are some berths, exposed to the loch, in front of the Clansman Hotel, a wooden Scandinavian-style building at the north side of the

bay. Showers and fresh water are available.

A charge is made in both cases, and a complimentary mini-bus service operates to Drumnadrochit, where there are stores.

Further south at Foyers (57°15'·5N 04°29'·3W), on the opposite side of the Loch, there is a quay where yachts may moor.

At Invermoriston (57°12'·4N 04°35'·3W) the bay may be shallow enough to anchor off the pier.

Fort Augustus at the SW end of Loch Ness has extensive stagings in the cut leading to a swing bridge and a staircase of 5 locks.

The first locking at Fort Augustus on Monday is to the westward.

A winding section of canal, about 6M long with isolated locks at Kytra and Cullochy, leads to a swing bridge at the end of Loch Oich.

Loch Oich, in contrast to Loch Ness, is narrow and shallow with bays and wooded islands, shingle beaches, and a marked channel. Towards the SW end, on the NW side a visitors pontoon is installed beside a general store at the Well of the Heads (57°20'N 04°27'W). The name refers to a gruesome incident in a clan feud.

This loch is only 3½M long, but there are many places to anchor. A development of holiday chalets at the SW end, The Great Glen Water Park, has a jetty at which to moor.

Just east of the Water Park, on the northwest shore there is a pontoon with 2m at its head, which is convenient for Invergarry Hotel. Note the level of Loch Oich may fall by nearly 0·3m when the river is scoured using loch water.

Another swing bridge crosses the canal at the north end of Laggan Avenue, a tree-lined section leading to Laggan Locks which drop down to Loch Lochy. beyond the locks, in a bay on the west side, a pontoon for visitors is provided. Part of this bay is shallow, and the depth must be carefully watched – see also the note below.

Loch Lochy is deep and steep-sided, like a smaller version of Loch Ness. Two hotels on the SE side have jetties where customers may moor, and there are several bays towards the south end of the NW side where it is possible to anchor, in particular at Achnacarry Bay (56°56'·4N 04°48'·5W).

Note that the level of Loch Lochy is controlled by a hydro-electric power station and there may be substantial fluctuations in water level.

At Gairlochy, about 9M from Laggan Locks, two locks lead to a 6-mile section of canal, in which Moy swing bridge is operated by a member of the canal staff who comes on a bicycle – so don't expect him to be waiting for you if you have stopped on the way! If you plan to stop tell the lock-keeper at the beginning of this section.

At Banavie, at the end of this section, is the famous Neptune's Staircase of 8 locks, with plenty of space to moor above them. Below the locks swing bridges for the railway and a main road may cause delays.

A further mile leads to Corpach, where a pair of locks drops to Corpach Basin and the Sea Lock. There are stagings for mooring above the pair of locks. It is not advisable, and the lock-keeper may not let you, to moor in the basin.

At the sea lock there is a staging with a pontoon at which to wait if entering from seaward.

Supplies

Apart from Inverness there are shops at Drumnadrochit, 1M from Urquhart Bay on Loch Ness; Invermoriston, Loch Ness; Fort Augustus; The Well of the Heads on Loch Oich; the Water Park development on Loch Oich; Corpach.

Thomasina on Loch Lochy, with the Ben Nevis range beyond

VIII. Tarbat Ness to Duncansby Head

The distance from Kinnaird Head to Wick is about 57M and to Duncansby Head is some 65M. From Tarbat Ness to Wick is about 42M.

Dangers and marks

Tarbat Ness lighthouse, white with red bands, stands east of the Dornoch Firth.

Culloden Rock, 2 cables NE of Tarbat Ness, was formerly marked by a buoy, which has been deleted.

Dunrobin Castle, and the Sutherland Monument on the skyline west of it, stand about 9M NW of Tarbat Ness.

Beatrice Oil Field, with several production platforms, lies about 13M off Dunbeath on the NW coast of the Moray Firth.

No.3 Y spar light buoy lies 13M southeast of the Beatrice Oil Field in approx. 2°50'W.

A radio mast north of Helmsdale stands 17M north of Tarbat Ness.

Clyth Ness lighthouse stands 16M NE of Helmsdale.

For the approach to the Moray Firth from seaward see the beginning of Chapter VII.

Dornoch Firth

58°51'N 04°00'W

Sailors from the shallow waters of the Thames Estuary may feel particularly at home here, although it lacks the mud and industrial waste.

Places of interest are the ancient town of Dornoch, and a distillery at Tain, but there are no convenient anchorages.

Charts

BA *223* (1:75,000). An old chart, *2170* (1:25,000), with depths in feet, may give some help but it must be emphasised that the sandbanks change constantly (see Appendix II). OS Explorer *438*.

Dangers and marks

Drying, and shifting, banks and shoals extend 4M from Dornoch Point, the north point of the entrance, to Tain Bar and continue within the firth.

A yellow spar buoy lies a mile north of Tarbat Ness.

Culloden Rock, 2 cables northeast of Tarbat Ness, was formerly marked by a buoy, which has been deleted.

Tain Bar buoy has been deleted.

A bombing range lies on the south side of the entrance.

A target float lies about 3½M west of Tarbat Ness.

A bridge with headroom of 11m lies across the firth, 3M west of Dornoch Point.

Tides

Constant –0140 Aberdeen (+0035 Dover)

Heights in metres

MHWS	MHWN	MTL	MLWN	MLWS
4·4	3·4	2·5	1·5	0·6

Lights

Tarbat Ness LtHo Fl(4)30s53m24M
Yellow spar-buoy Fl.Y.5s
Target Float Fl.Y.5s

Portmahomack

⊕ 1 cable NW of pier head 58°50'·3N 03°50'W

A fishing village with some shelter from south and east, and from north behind a drying pier, but berths alongside are usually all occupied by resident fishing boats. May be disturbed by aircraft using a bombing range at Tain.

Tides

Constant –0130 Aberdeen (+0100 Dover)

Heights in metres

MHWS	MHWN	MTL	MLWN	MLWS
4·1	3·3	2·5	1·7	0·7

Distances

Cromarty 15M, Burghead 17M, Helmsdale 18M.

Dangers

Curach Rocks which dry 0·8m lie up to a cable SW of the pier, and reefs extend a cable from the shore north of the pier.

See also Dornoch Firth, above.

Approach

From south give Tarbat Ness a berth of half a mile to avoid Culloden Rock.

From north keep ¼M off shore until west of the pier head, and turn to head for it, keeping a good

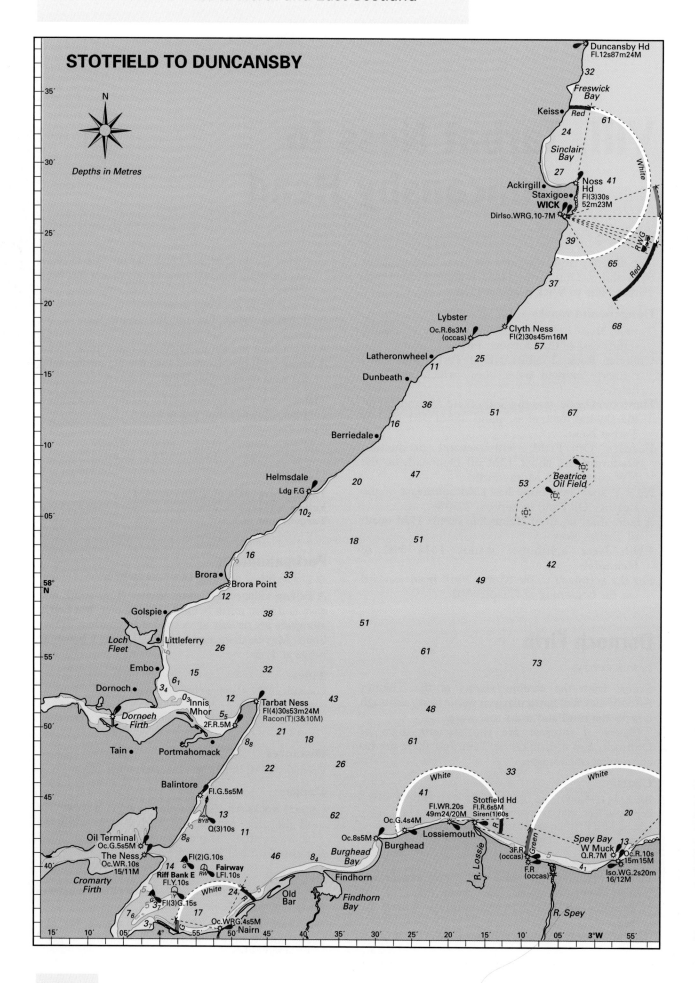

STOTFIELD TO DUNCANSBY

N

Depths in Metres

Duncansby Hd
Fl.12s87m24M

32

Freswick
Bay

Keiss • Red

61

24

Sinclair
Bay

27

White

Ackirgill •

Noss 41
Hd
Staxigoe • Fl(3)30s
52m23M

WICK •

DirIso.WRG.10-7M

RWG

39

Red

37

65

68

Lybster
Oc.R.6s3M
(occas)

Clyth Ness
Fl(2)30s45m16M

57

Latheronwheel

25

Dunbeath • 11

36

51

67

Berriedale • 16

Beatrice
Oil Field

Helmsdale • 53

Ldg F.G

47

20

51

42

18

10₂

16

Brora • 33

49

Brora Point

12

38

Golspie •

51

Loch
Fleet

Littleferry •

26

61

Embo • 15

32

73

6₁

Dornoch • 3₄

0₃

Innis
Mhor 12

Tarbat Ness
Fl(4)30s53m24M
Racon(T)(3&10M)

43

48

5₅

2F.R.5M

21

18

61

Dornoch
Firth

8₈

Tain • Portmahomack •

22

26

Balintore • 33

White

White

Fl.G.5s5M

41

Stotfield Hd
Fl.R.6s5M
Siren(1)60s

20

BYB

13

Q(3)10s 11

62

Fl.WR.20s
49m24/20M

Spey Bay
W Muck 13

Oil Terminal
Oc.G.5s5M

8₈

46

8₄

Oc.G.4s4M

Oc.8s5M

Lossiemouth

R. Lossie

3F.R.
(occas)

Green

5

Oc.R.10s
15m15M

The Ness
Oc.WR.10s
15/11M

14

Fl(2)G.10s

Burghead

R

F.R
(occas)

Q.R.7M

4₁

Iso.WG.2s20m
16/12M

Cromarty
Firth

Riff Bank E
Fl.Y.10s

RW

Fairway
LFl.10s

Burghead
Bay

Findhorn

R. Spey

5

White

24

R

Old
Bar

Findhorn
Bay

5₅

Fl(3)G.15s

17

7₆

Oc.WRG.4s5M

3₇

Nairn

Portmahomack. Curach Rocks are unmarked and do not show in this photo

lookout for Curach Rocks which may not show in quiet weather, but are usually marked by fishing floats.

Anchorage

Clear of Curach Rocks, or further SW in W or SW wind.

Lights

Pier head 2F.R(vert)5M

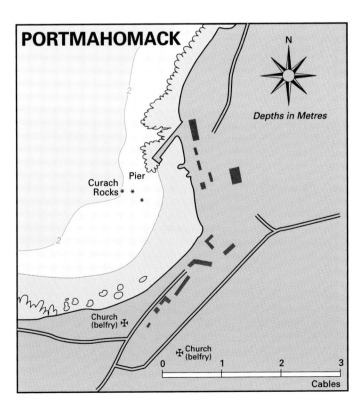

PORTMAHOMACK

N

Depths in Metres

Curach
Rocks * * *

Pier

Church
(belfry) ✠

✠ Church
(belfry)

0   1   2   3

Cables

Shelter

Is reasonable in winds between east and southwest. If space is available visiting yachts may dry out alongside the pier.

Supplies

Water at pier. Diesel and petrol at garage. Shop, PO, telephone, hotel in village.

Embo Pier

57°54'·1N 03°59'·4W

A stone pier extends south from the shore at Embo Point, north of the entrance to Dornoch Firth, 8M WNW of Tarbat Ness.

Supplies

Water, shop, *Calor Gas*, telephone, café, at nearby caravan site.

Littleferry

⊕ on leading line at 5m contour 57°55'·7N 03°59'W

The narrow entrance to Loch Fleet, an extensive lagoon which largely dries. It is a bird reserve, managed by SNH.

Distances

Portmahomack 8M, Helmsdale 18M.

Tides

As Dornoch Firth.
Streams in the narrows run at least 2½ knots

Dangers and marks

Drying sands extend seaward 4 cables on either side of the channel.

Littleferry and Loch Fleet

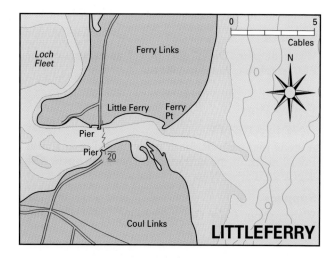

LITTLEFERRY

A bar with a depth of 0·6m lies ½M from the shore. Power cables with a safe headroom of 20m cross the channel; the pylons are conspicuous.

Approach

Keep one mile offshore until the entrance has been identified. There are now no leading marks but in the channel the power cable pylon bears approx. 295°. Do not approach before half flood; this should obviously only be attempted in very quiet weather.

Shelter

May be found on the west side of the south point of the entrance. Crews of local shellfish dredgers are reported to be hostile to yachts.

Golspie

57°58'·2N 03°58'·7W

A stone pier with an L-shaped head, lying to the south of the village, gives some protection from the north and may be approached above half tide. The bottom south of the pier is clean sand and some local boats are kept on running moorings. The

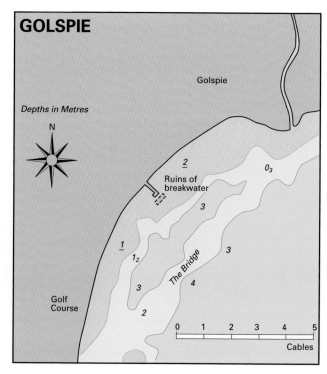

GOLSPIE

Golspie Pier

construction of the pier makes it unsuitable for berthing alongside without constant supervision.

The remains of a breakwater lies submerged off the head of the pier on a line parallel with the shore, and a post is reported to stand at its south end.

An Drochaid (the bridge), a shingle bank, part of which just dries, lies ¼M offshore. For the deepest water across the bridge steer with the Sutherland Monument bearing 316° until a church spire in the village bears about 006°, and steer on that line. A boathouse which used to define the first line has long ceased to exist. Slipway at root of pier.

Tides

Heights in metres

MHWS	MHWN	MTL	MLWN	MLWS
4·0	3·1	2·3	1·5	0·6

Supplies

Shops (including gas), PO, hotels; no water or fuel.

Brora

58°00'·7N 03°50'·5W

A drying river mouth harbour only approachable near HW, and only if there is no sea running.

Tides

The flood tide runs SSW across the entrance.

Distances

Portmahomack 10M, Helmsdale 9M.

Dangers and marks

A drying reef on the south side of the entrance may be marked by a red can buoy.

A steep shingle bank on the north side is marked by a post standing inshore of the LW line.

A bar with a drying bank in mid-channel lies across the entrance.

Leading marks on the south shore consisting of white poles with red tops lead through the deepest water south of the mid-channel bank.

A railway bridge across the river east of the harbour is conspicuous.

Lights

None.

Shelter

Is good once inside the bar.

Approach

Local opinion is divided between approaching only within an hour of HW, or within two hours; one fisherman commented that the bank is gravel and if you do trip over it you can wait until the tide rises and will come to no harm! Approach only if no sea is running.

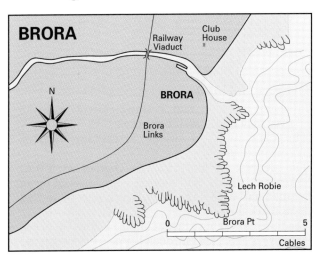

Brora

Supplies

Petrol and diesel at garage. Shops, PO, telephone, hotel in town. Train to Wick and south. Distillery.

Helmsdale

58°07'N 03°39'W

The approach has a bar with drying banks on either side. Pontoons have been provided for visiting yachts. Do not attempt to approach the old harbour at the road bridge.

Tides

Constant –0000 Aberdeen (+0035 Dover)

Heights in metres

MHWS	MHWN	MTL	MLWN	MLWS
3·9	3·1	2·3	1·5	0·7

Distances

Buckie 34M, Wick 29M.

Dangers and marks

In spring and after rain a strong current from the river may be felt well out to sea.

The concrete road bridge across the river is conspicuous.

The deepest water (currently charted as 1·0m) between drying banks on the bar is marked by an unlit starboard-hand buoy, which may be moved to mark the best water.

Leading marks consisting of orange boards on posts, bearing 313°, lead through the deepest water over the bar.

Lights

Ldg Lts F.G (front light F.R when harbour is closed)

Approach

Identify the leading marks and buoy, satisfy yourself that there is enough depth of water in relation to any sea running and follow this line across the bar.

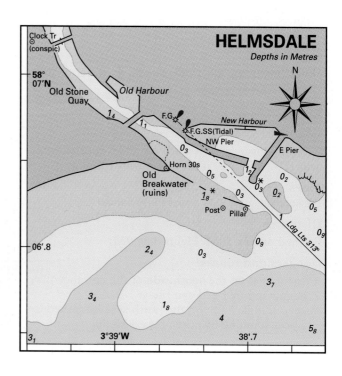

Helmsdale (before installation of pontoons)

Shelter

Is good when inside. Berth at pontoons on north side of harbour.

Supplies

Water at quay. Diesel by road tanker. Shops, PO, telephone, hotel in town. Slipway.

Between Helmsdale and Wick, a distance of 30M, there are several small harbours none of which except Lybster is suitable for a deep keel yacht.

The tide along the coast runs at a rate of up to one knot.

Harbourmaster VHF Ch 12.

Berriedale

58°11'N 03°29'W

A river-mouth sheltered from southeast, which provided a landing place in the days of sailing coasters, and only of interest to owners of *Crabbers*, *Luggers* and RIBs. A sand bar is reported to lie across the entrance. Not recommended without intimate local knowledge.

Berriedale was a landing place for coasters in the days of sail

Dunbeath

58°14'·5N 03°25'W

Dunbeath Castle, a conspicuous white house, stands on a promontory on the south side of the bay.

A power cable to Beatrice oil field runs out from two beacons at the head of the bay.

The harbour, which dries, occupies the mouth of a river on the north side of the bay.

Drying rocks extend more than half a cable off shore east of the harbour.

Boulders are sometimes carried down the river in spate.

The head of the west breakwater is foul with submerged debris.

A depth of at least 0·7m can be expected inside the entrance, but submerged concrete shelves project in places from the east breakwater.

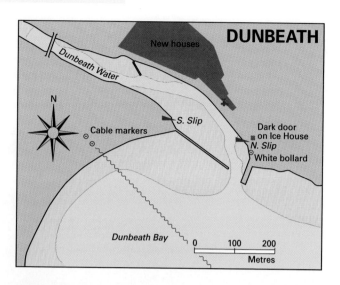

Approach

Keeping closer to the east breakwater, with a white bollard on the quay ahead in line with the dark door of an icehouse bearing about 018°.

Berth temporarily and check that the berth is not allocated to a permanent berth-holder. The berth on the east pier is allocated to a full-time working fishing boat, and part of the quay wall to the west of the leading line is marked 'No Mooring' as the local authority considers it unsound.

Supplies

Hotel, shop (inc. *Calor Gas*) ½M north. PO 1M south. Garage (1½M north) may provide mechanic (no petrol).

Dunbeath

Latheronwheel (Janetstown)

58°16'N 03°22'W

A drying harbour with a sandy bottom, only fit for small boats. Sometimes congested in summer with local boats.

Approach

With end of south pier in line with chimney on gable end of old bothy (shed) at south side of river mouth.

Hotel currently closed, general store closed, butcher's shop at Latheron, 1M. No fuel (petrol or diesel) for 2½M either way on main road.

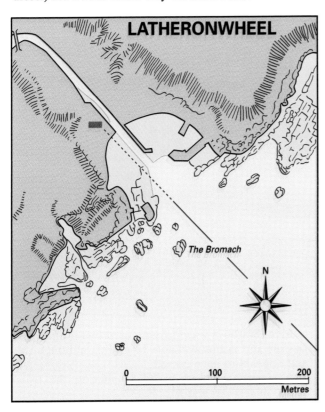

Latheronwheel

Lybster

58°17'N 03°17'W

Usable by keelboats in moderate conditions and providing complete shelter in the inner basin, although the entrance is narrow (10m).

Tides

Constant −0200 Aberdeen (+0020 Dover)

Heights in metres

MHWS	MHWN	MTL	MLWN	MLWS
3·5	2·8	2·2	1·6	0·7

Distances

Wick 12M, Buckie 38M, Helmsdale 16M.

Dangers and marks

Seas in the entrance are steep in quite moderate onshore winds.

A white lighthouse on the pier head is conspicuous.

Approach

With the lighthouse bearing about 350°.

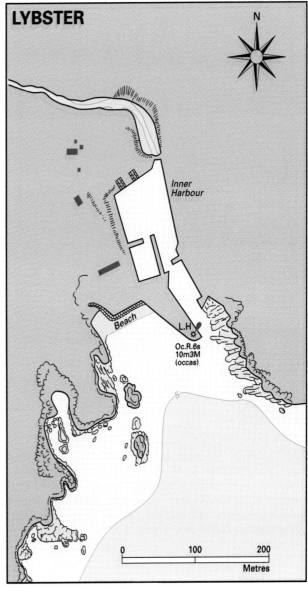

Lybster

Lights

LtHo Oc.R.6s10m3M may only be shown when fishing boats are at sea.

Shelter

Is excellent in the inner basin, where the depth is 1·2m, mud.

Supplies

Water on south quay, shop, PO, telephone, hotel ½M.

Harbourmaster ☎ 01593 721325.

Wick

⊕ on leading line 58°26'·3N 03°03'·8W

Distances

Fraserburgh 57M, Helmsdale 27M, Duncansby Head 13M, Scrabster 31M.

An artificial harbour at a river mouth providing complete shelter once inside, but the approach is hazardous in easterly winds of more than F6. The ruins of a breakwater extending from the south shore, mostly submerged, show that even the Stevensons could not always control the power of the sea.

River Harbour was formerly used by oil rig supply vessels and is not available to yachts, although this use appears to have ceased.

A secure enclosed harbour, offering the usual range of services and supplies.

Charts

BA *115* (1:200,000), *1462* (plan); Imray *C22* and *C68*; OS Landranger *12*.

Tides

Constant −0220 Aberdeen (+0010 Dover)
Heights in metres

MHWS	MHWN	MTL	MLWN	MLWS
3·5	2·8	2·1	1·4	0·7

Dangers and marks

The head of the ruined breakwater which extends more than a cable from the south side of the bay is marked by an unlit north cardinal beacon.

Drying rocks extend a cable SE from North Head.

Approach

In the centre of the bay, keeping a lookout for working vessels, and the beacon at the end of the ruined breakwater.

Turn to enter Outer Harbour as soon as the entrance is seen, as the water on the NW side of the channel is very shoal, but look out for vessels coming out which may be hidden by the breakwater.

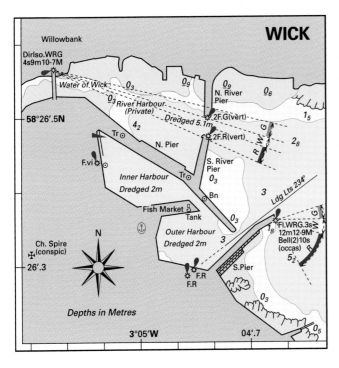

Lights

Floodlights 32m high stand on North Pier
Head of River Harbour DirIso.WRG.4s9m10-7M
South pier Fl.WRG.3s12m12-9M
The entrance to River Harbour is marked by 2F.R(vert) light on its south side and 2F.G(vert) light on its north side.
Ldg Lts 234° F.R into Outer Harbour

At night

Any sector of the DirIso light at the head of River Harbour, as well as the white sector of South Pier light leads clear of rocks and the ruined breakwater. Look out for leading lights as soon as South Pier light is abeam, and turn to bring them in line to avoid the shoal water.

Supplies

Water, diesel, petrol, boatyard, chandlery and showers at harbour. *Calor Gas*, shops, PO, telephone, hotels, launderette, in town. Rail, air, and bus services.

Harbourmaster VHF Ch 14 or ☎ 01955 602030.

Wick

Staxigoe

Staxigoe

58°27'N 03°03'W

An inlet a mile north of the entrance to Wick Bay, a traditional fishing station which may be suitable for a brief stop for stores in quiet weather. Wick is some 1½M by road.

Passage notes

The tide runs strongly along the coast between Wick Bay and Noss Head, 2½M further north, and the sea may be very disturbed with wind against tide. On a passage south your troubles may not be over when you have passed Duncansby Head.

The NNE-going stream begins −0040 Aberdeen (+0140 Dover).

The SSW-going stream begins +0530 Aberdeen (−0435 Dover.

Sinclair Bay provides some shelter in offshore winds, and the south side may be particularly welcome during southerly winds while waiting for the flood tide to turn.

Ackergill

58°29'N 03°06'W

On the south side of Sinclair Bay, provides some shelter from southerly winds.

The stone jetty appears to have 2·5m alongside at half tide; approach on the line of the outer leg of the jetty to avoid off-lying submerged and drying reefs, or anchor off.

Anchor 1–1½ cables off the pier unless attempting to go alongside.

The structure on the west side is a former lifeboat slip.

Supplies

None, but Wick is 2M by road.

Keiss

⊕ on leading line 58°32'N 03°07'W

A fine stone harbour built by Bremner in the early part of the 19th century, currently used by a few inshore fishing boats.

The entrance is very tight with a sharp right-angled turn through a gap only 9m wide into the inner basin.

A depth of 1m may be expected in the harbour entrance.

Ackergill

In southerly and easterly winds the sea in the outer basin makes manoeuvring hazardous.

A short breakwater (which covers) at the east side of the entrance is marked by a perch.

A white square painted on the face of a stone warehouse, showing over the entrance leads in to the harbour.

Berth alongside a stone quay in the drying inner harbour or, in settled weather, in the outer harbour.

Supplies

General store, water at spring.

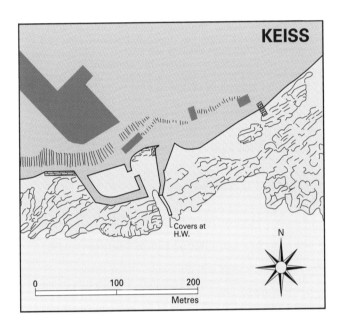

Keiss

Freswick Bay

58°35'·5N 03°03'·5W

Freswick Bay provides shelter in offshore winds, but if the wind is fair the only reason to delay a passage north would be if Duncansby Race is expected to be excessively rough. In this case a more suitable place to wait might be Ackergill (above). Excellent landing (in northerly wind) at a stone jetty at Skirza Haven on the north side of the bay. Telephone ½M towards main road.

Tidal streams

An eddy sets into Freswick Bay, and the north-going stream begins +0420 Aberdeen (−0545 Dover).
The south-going stream begins +0055 Aberdeen (+0315 Dover).

Charts

OS Explorer *451* covers coast from Keiss to Thurso

Skirza

IX. North coast of Scotland

The north coast of Scotland is not a place for the faint-hearted or the inexperienced. Over 60M of rock-bound coast extends from the Pentland Firth, through which run the strongest tidal streams in Britain, to Cape Wrath. In that distance there is only one sheltered deep-water harbour (Scrabster), 16M west of Duncansby Head, together with a selection of anchorages in two lochs near the west end, and a few boat harbours and occasional anchorages in between. There is a wealth of coves and bays which might be explored with a small boat, but little shelter if it turns rough.

This spectacular coast has been a highway throughout European history from the Vikings onwards. A naval action was fought in the Jacobite actions of 1745 in the Kyle of Tongue, between a French and an English ship, both of which were commanded by Irishmen.

Pentland Firth

Pentland Firth, between Orkney Is and mainland Scotland, is subject to very strong tides with overfalls and tide races at specific locations. There are certain times only, even under favourable conditions, when these hazards may be safely negotiated.

On a passage to the west coast a tactical decision needs to be made before entering the Moray Firth, whether to take the Caledonian Canal, or tackle the Pentland Firth. At a later stage you can still decide to pass among the Orkney Islands where the tides, although still strong, are less fierce.

Other things being equal, the passage through the Pentland Firth is less hazardous from west to east.

The area is especially prone to fog in May and June.

Charts

BA *1954* (1:200,000), *2162* (1:50,000), *2581* (1:26,000); OS Landranger *12*; OS Explorer *451*

Dangers and marks

Muckle Skerry, the largest of the Pentland Skerries, is identified by a conspicuous lighthouse.

Duncansby Head has a stumpy lighthouse on top of a cliff.

Drying and submerged rocks lie up to 2 cables offshore between Duncansby Head and Dunnet Head.

Stroma Skerries, south of the southwest point of Stroma, are marked by a YB beacon 12m in height with a port-hand topmark.

Men of Mey Rocks, a drying reef, extends 2 cables north of St John's Point.

Tides

Note that on Admiralty Charts in Pentland Firth tidal streams are related to Aberdeen, but from Dunnet Head westward they are related to Ullapool. On chart *1954* and on Imray's *C68* all tidal streams are related to Ullapool, but on BA chart *2162* they are related to Aberdeen.

Eddies form on the lee side of each island and headland with severe overfalls off the headlands and the points of each island.

Between Duncansby Head and the Pentland Skerries:

The east-going stream begins about +0505 Aberdeen (–0500 Dover).

The west-going stream begins about –0105 Aberdeen (+0115 Dover).

Spring rates are about 8 knots, but near Pentland Skerries streams of 12 knots are common.

Duncansby Race forms on the flood, extending from Ness of Duncansby (a mile WNW of Duncansby Head) to Pentland Skerries beginning at +0245 Aberdeen (+0505 Dover).

It dies away between +0430 and +0505 Aberdeen (–0535 and –0500 Dover).

The race then rotates anti-clockwise, and at –0440 Aberdeen (–0220 Dover) it extends NW towards Boars of Duncansby, where the seas break.

It dies away with the beginning of the west-going stream at –0105 Aberdeen (+0115 Dover).

In the firth generally:

The east-going stream begins +0500 Aberdeen (–0505 Dover).

The west-going stream begins –0130 Aberdeen (+0050 Dover).

The Swilkie race lies off the north end of Stroma, and eddies form on its downstream side, in either case with north-going streams along the shore.

In Inner Sound

The west-going stream begins about –0150 Aberdeen (+0030 Dover).

The east-going stream begins about +0435 Aberdeen (–0530 Dover).

Spring rates are about 5 knots, but increase off Stroma Skerries.

In the west part of the firth, on the south side, at a point ½M north of Dunnet Head the tide turns significantly earlier, as follows:

The east-going stream begins +0240 Aberdeen (+0500 Dover).

The west-going stream begins –0320 Aberdeen (–0100 Dover)

The Merry Men of Mey, the most dangerous race in the Pentland Firth, extends from St John's Point to Tor Ness on Hoy.

The race begins to form about –0150 Aberdeen (+0030 Dover) with the west-going stream. It reaches its full strength about +0200 Aberdeen and extends across the full width of the Firth.

About +0315 Aberdeen a passage begins to open between the Men of Mey rocks and the south end of the race.

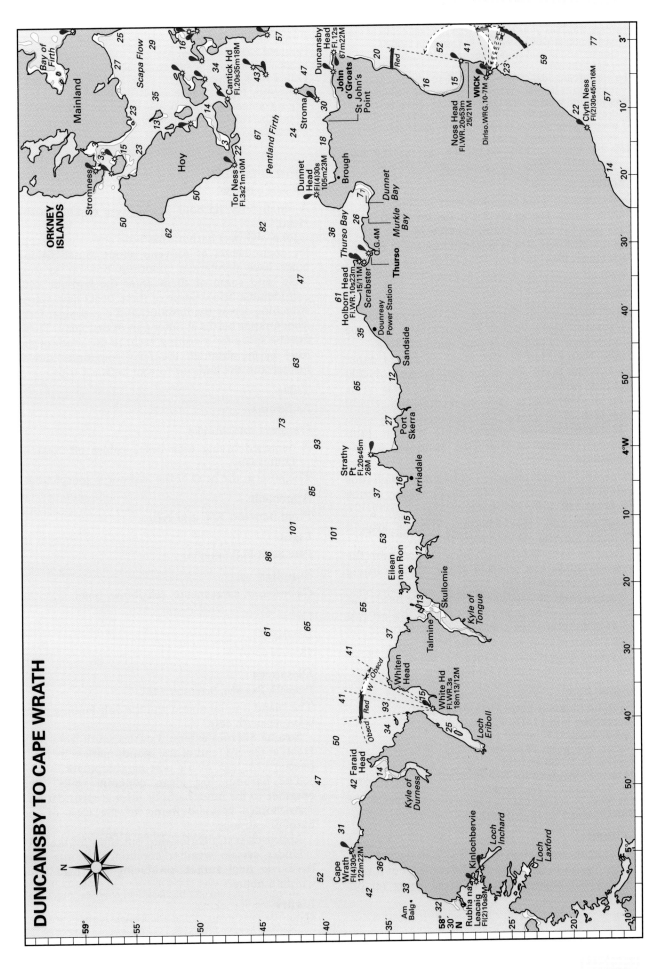

DUNCANSBY TO CAPE WRATH

ORKNEY
ISLANDS

Bay of
Firth

Mainland

Scapa Flow

Cantick Hd
Fl.20s35m18M

Stromness

Hoy

Tor Ness
Fl.3s21m10M

Pentland Firth

Stroma

St John's
Point

John
o'Groats

Duncansby
Head
Fl.12s
67m22M

Dunnet
Head
Fl(4)30s
105m23M

Brough

Dunnet
Bay

Murkle
Bay

Thurso Bay

Q.G.4M

Thurso

Scrabster

Holborn Head
Fl.WR.10s23m
15/11M

Dounreay
Power Station

Sandside

Port
Skerra

Strathy
Pt
Fl.20s45m
26M

Arriadale

Eilean
nan Ron

Skullomie

Kyle of
Tongue

Talmine

Whiten
Head

White Hd
Fl.WR.3s
18m13/12M

Loch
Eriboll

Faraid
Head

Kyle of
Durness

Cape
Wrath
Fl(4)30s
122m22M

Am
Balg

Rubha na
Leacaig
Fl(2)10s8M

Kinlochbervie

Loch
Inchard

Loch
Laxford

WICK

Noss Head
Fl.WR.20s53m
25/21M

Dirlso.WRG.10-7M

Clyth Ness
Fl(2)30s45m16M

N

Obscd

Red

W Obscd

Obscd   Red

The race subsides at its NW end with the beginning of the
east-going stream about +0435 Aberdeen (+0030
Dover), and in mid-stream about +0515 Aberdeen
(−0450 Dover).

The west-going tidal stream can reach 10 knots raising
tumultuous overfalls, especially with wind against tide.

Passage from west to east with a fair tide presents less
problem, except for the strength of the tide, and the
need to keep clear of the Men of Mey and the Swilkie,
which is particularly strong on the flood.

Note that eddies run northward on the west side of Brough
Bay and Gills Bay.

Shelter

Depending on wind direction, may be found in:
Freswick Bay, 4M south of Duncansby Head.
Gills Bay 4M west of Duncansby Head.
Stroma Harbour, 3M WNW of Duncansby Head.
Aith Hope, Hoy, Orkney, 10M NNW of Duncansby
Head.

Directions

From southeast if the tide is unfavourable at
Duncansby Head wait at Freswick Bay, or if the
wind is easterly and too strong, stand offshore.

The Merry Men of Mey must be passed either
towards the north side of the firth between −0200
and HW Aberdeen, or at the south side clear of the
Men of Mey Rocks between +0330 and +0430
Aberdeen.

If conditions are unfavourable wait at John
o'Groats, Stroma or Gills Bay, according to tide
conditions.

From east and northeast note Liddel Eddy which runs
west along the south side of South Ronaldsay during
the latter half of the east-going stream.

From west note that SE-going streams around
Pentland Skerries are extremely strong.

Heading eastward through Inner Sound from the
west advantage can be taken of the stream turning
earlier off Dunnet Head.

Pass as close as conditions allow to the head, and
aim to arrive off St John's Point during the last two
hours of the ebb when a space opens up between the
Merry Men of Mey race and the point.

To keep clear of hazards inshore further east, keep
Dunnet Head open of St John's Point.

Lights

Pentland Skerries LtHo Fl(3)30s52m23M
Duncansby Head LtHo Fl.12s67m22M
Lother Rock Q.13m6M
Swona, SW point Fl.8s17m9M
N point Fl(3)10s16m10M
Swilkie Point, Stroma Fl(2)20s32m26M Horn(2)60s
Cantick Head Fl.20s35m18M
Tor Ness Fl.3s21m10M
Dunnet Head Fl(4)30s105m23M

At night

These lights are enough to guide a yacht through the
Outer Sound in fair (and clear) weather, but a very
close watch must be kept to avoid being set off
course.

Fog signals, radio and radar beacons

Pentland Skerries – Horn 45s
Swilkie Point, Stroma – Horn (2) 60s
Lother Rock – Racon
Duncansby Head – Racon and Radio beacon
Fog is common and may be patchy, so that it appears
unexpectedly. Propagation of sound signals is very
uneven in fog.

John o'Groats

58°39'N 03°04'W

A small ferry harbour 1½M west of Duncansby
Head.

John o'Groats harbour has little attraction, except
for connoisseurs of souvenir shops. Small fishing
boats have permanent moorings bow-on to west
quay (and some of them enter the harbour with
considerable brio). Some of these boats have warps
stretching across the harbour, and a passenger ferry
from Orkney berths at outer part of east quay. There
may be space for a visiting yacht to the south of the
ferry berth, although the ferry sometimes moves
further into the harbour to wait between trips.

Tides

As Stroma.

Dangers and marks

A detached drying rock lies 2 cables off Ness of
Duncansby.
The hotel at the head of the harbour is conspicuous.

Approach

From between NW and NE.

Light

Pier head Fl.R.3s4m2M

Supplies

Calor Gas at caravan site, telephone, hotel.

Stroma

58°40'N 03°07'W

Distances

Freswick Bay 8M, Scrabster 15M.

The island is uninhabited and the only landing place
is on its south side.

Stroma Skerries extend 2 cables south from Mell
Head at the SW end of the island, marked by a YB
beacon 12m high with a port-hand topmark.

The harbour has clean concrete walls. The
entrance to the inner harbour dries at chart datum.

Anchorage may be found to the west of the
harbour entrance.

Approach is straightforward but allow for the tide.

Under certain weather conditions Stroma may
have two tidal surges, producing two high tides
within 6 hours.

Lights

None.

John o'Groats

Supplies

None.

Tides

Constant −0455 Aberdeen (−0240 Dover)

Heights in metres

MHWS	MHWN	MTL	MLWN	MLWS
3·1	2·3	1·8	1·3	0·5

Stroma harbour

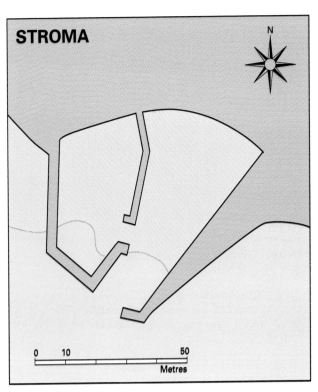

Harrow

Charts

BA old chart *1783* (1:14,280), see Appendix II; OS Explorer *451*

A north-facing bay with an L-shaped stone jetty on its west side, may be obstructed by a moored fishing boat with a network of warps.

Brough

Charts

BA old chart *1783* (1:14,280), see Appendix II; OS Explorer *451*

Anchorage off a concrete slip, partly sheltered by the Cletts, 25m high.

Dunnet Head is a cliff 102m high, with a white lighthouse.

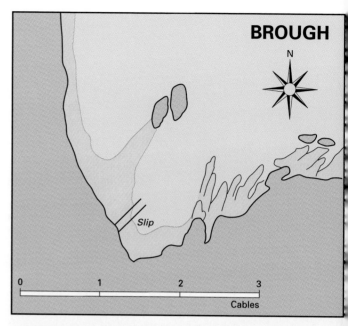

Harrow

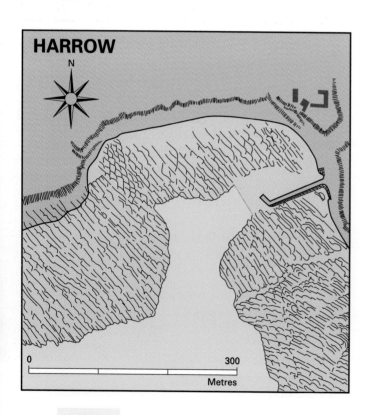

Brough

Tides

At a point ½M north of Dunnet Head

The west-going stream begins about +0320 Ullapool (−0100 Dover).

The east-going stream begins about −0305 Ullapool (+0500 Dover).

Dunnett Bay, on the west side of Dunnet Head, is one of the best locations in Britain for surfboarding, the conditions for which makes it unattractive for a visiting yacht.

Murkle

58°36'N 03°23'W

Charts

BA old chart *1783* (1:14,280), see Appendix II; OS Explorer *451*

If there is no north in the wind this bay, with a sheltering reef on the northeast side, provides an occasional anchorage.

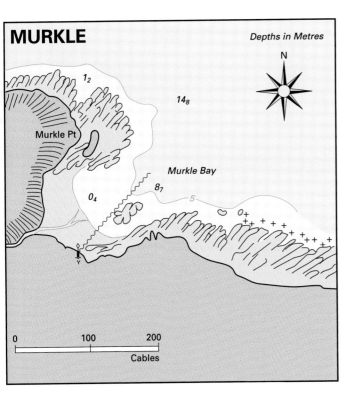

Murkle Bay

Note that a submarine cable extends northeast from a beacon on the beach, and a detached reef lies in the south part of the bay.

Dwarwick

Charts

BA old chart *1783* (1:14,280), see Appendix II; OS Explorer *451*

A stone pier on the north side of Dunnet Bay.

Castlehill
58°36'N 03°23'W

Charts

BA old chart *1783* (1:14,280), see Appendix II; OS Explorer *451*

A small drying artificial harbour on the south side of Dunnet Bay, originally built about 1820 for the export of Caithness flagstones (Norse *flaga*); the associated buildings are being restored and a Flagstone Trail has been established.

Fishing boats are moored with a network of lines to keep them clear of the wall, which may leave little space for a visitor.

Supplies

In Castletown village, about ½M.

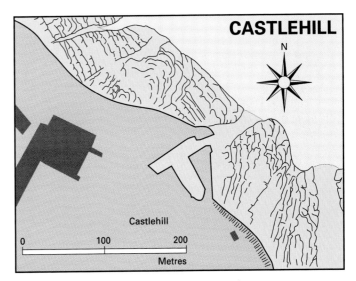

Castlehill

Thurso

58°36'N 03°31'W

The town and harbour stand at the mouth of Thurso River on the south side of Thurso Bay, with drying reefs on either side of the channel.

Leading lights on inconspicuous posts lead in to the entrance.

The quayside to starboard almost dries.

Lights

Ldg Lts 195° F.G
(A light on the breakwater Q.G is only shown from September to April)

Supplies

Water, shops, diesel, petrol at garages. Rail and bus connections.

Scrabster

58°37'N 03°33'W

A fishing and commercial harbour in the SW corner of Thurso Bay with depth at all states of tide, suitable for a deep-keel cruising yacht.

Charts

BA *1462* (1:10,000)(plan); Imray chart *C68* (plan)

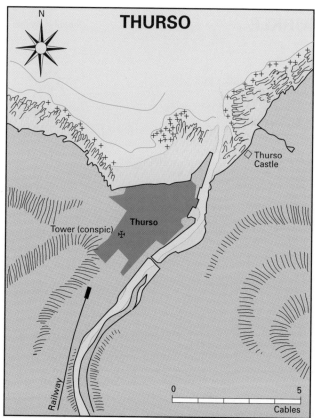

Thurso

Thurso

Distances

Wick 31M, Talmine 30M.

Tides

Constant –0455 Aberdeen (–0210 Dover)

Heights in metres

MHWS	MHWN	MTL	MLWN	MLWS
4·0	3·7	2·9	2·1	0·8

Approach

Straightforward, but take care to avoid mistaking Thurso for Scrabster.

The ice plant tower is conspicuous.

Call harbourmaster before entering.

Lights

Dunnet head Fl(4)30s105m23M
Holborn head Fl.WR.10s23m15/11M
Outer pier head Q(2)G.8m4M
South breakwater head Q.R.6m4M

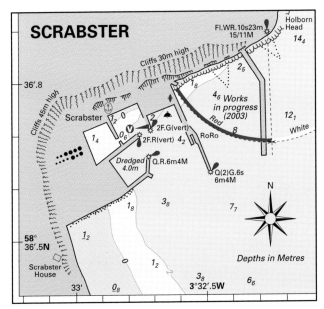

Ice quay 2F.G(vert)
Tanker berth 2F.R(vert)

Supplies and services

Water at South Wall fuel berth and Lay-by Quay, diesel at Fuel Berth. Petrol from garage, about 1M. *Calor Gas* at South Wall fuel berth, shops and supermarkets at Thurso (2M), PO, telephone, hotel, showers, chandlery. Fishermen's Mission. Ice.

Repairs to hull and machinery. Mobile cranes.

Bus service to Thurso, Inverness and south. Rail service from Thurso. Air services from Wick, ferry to Orkney and occasional service to Bergen and Faeroe.

Harbourmaster VHF Ch 12, ☎ 01847 892779. Office at north side of Central Dock.

Holborn Head to Whiten Head

Charts

BA *1954* (1:200,000); OS Landranger *10-12*

As there is no large-scale chart for the coast west of Scrabster other than that for Loch Eriboll, small boats exploring inshore might find the OS Explorer 1:25,000 Nos. *447-449* useful.

Most of the plans in this chapter have been compiled from Admiralty surveys, which date from the 1840s.

The distance from Scrabster to Talmine, the principal anchorage at Kyle of Tongue, is 30M.

Dangers and marks

Holborn Head is a cliff 30m high.

Dounreay nuclear establishment is identified by a conspicuous sphere.

Strathy Point stands 35m high with a white lighthouse.

Scrabster. A new RoRo terminal is being built at the right since this photo was taken

Tides

At a point ½M north of Holborn Head

The west-going stream begins about +0420 Ullapool (HW Dover).

The east-going stream begins about –0140 Ullapool (–0600 Dover).

The spring rate is about 3 knots.

Between Strathy Point and Whiten Head

The west-going stream begins about +0350 Ullapool (+0545 Dover).

The east-going stream begins about –0220 Ullapool (–0030 Dover).

The spring rate is about 3 knots.

At Strathy Point an eddy forms off the east side of the point with overfalls where the eddy meets the main stream.

Turbulence occurs wherever wind and tide are opposed and there will be steep seas.

Shelter

Some shelter may be found in offshore wind on either side of Strathy Point to wait for slack water or a fair tide.

Lights

Holborn head Fl.WR.10s23m15/11M
Strathy Point Fl.20s45m26M

Sandside (Fresgoe)

58°34'N 03°47'W

A small boat harbour on the west side of Sandside Bay, facing the Dounreay nuclear research establishment.

The harbour dries completely but the bottom is clean sand.

Provisions, pub, PO, in Reay village, about a mile.

On the west side of Melvich Bay, a drying pier extends from the shore.

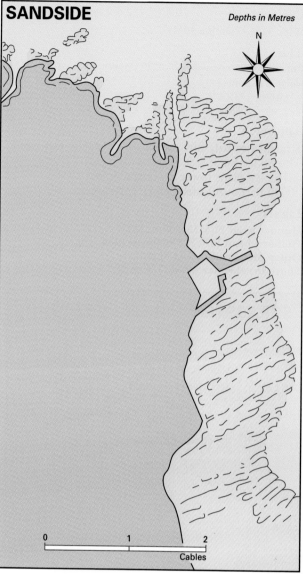

SANDSIDE — Depths in Metres

Sandside (Fresgoe) Harbour

Portskerra

58°34'N 03°55'W

A pool among skerries at the tip of Rubha Bhra, 3M ESE of Strathy Point, provides occasional anchorage for small boats, as well as permanent moorings for one or two local boats.

A broad detached rock, The Stag of Portskerra, which dries 2m, lies 1 cable N of Rubha Bra.

The plan is derived from a survey plan drawn by a member of Captain Otter's team in 1843.

Note particularly the broad rock drying 0·6m in the entrance; a remark on the survey plan advises 'to enter at low water keep close to the south rock, or within 10 yards of mid rock.'

Boursa

58°35'N 04°03'W

The creek behind Boursa Island, which is mentioned in successive editions of the Admiralty *Pilot*, provides some shelter from NE wind, in a pool

Portskerra from north

Boursa from east

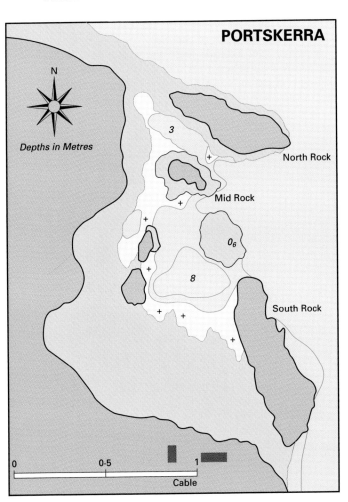

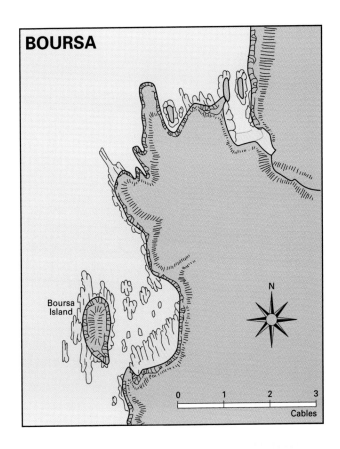

rather encumbered by drying rocks, entered by the south side of the island.

At least some shelter from NE would be found at the mouth of the inlet.

A clear channel lies close to the island, and SE of the large skerries, and a small fishing boat appears to

Boursa from southeast

have a permanent mooring at the head of the creek in the northeast corner.

Kirtomy
58°33'N 04°05'·7W

A small inlet sheltered from the west by a low island, with a drying reef close to the east, and a slip on the shore. Telephone ½M.

Torrisdale Bay
58°32'N 04°15'W

Anchorage in offshore wind. Boats can reach a drying pier at Bettyhill at half flood.

Caol Beag
58°32'·7N 04°18'W

Caol Beag has a clear passage on its northeast side, but drying reefs extend north from Skerray Bay.

Neave Island

This island, on the north side of Caol Beag, has an occasional anchorage in Bagh Gaineamheach, a sandy bay on SE side. Note the reef extending east from the south side of the bay.

Skerray Bay
58°32'N 04°19'W

Skerray Bay on the mainland SW of Neave Island has a stone pier on its west side, behind which local boats may be moored, but most of the harbour dries. The deepest water is at the east end, at the steps behind the head of the pier.

A drying reef extends from the west point of the bay, with a detached rock awash off the end and a drying reef extends northwest from the east side.

Torrisdale Bay

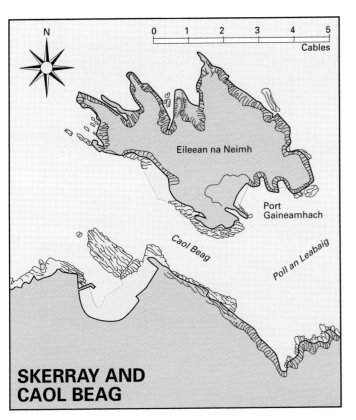

Skerray

SKERRAY AND CAOL BEAG

Skerray showing rocks on both sides of the channel just breaking

Approach

From NW, only in the quietest weather midway between the shore and the reef, keeping a lookout for the reefs shown on the photo, especially the one shown just breaking beyond the pier.

Lamigo Bay and **Port an t'Strathain,** west of Skerray, provide occasional anchorage in offshore wind.

Caol Raineach

58°32'·5N 04°21'W

The passage south of Eilean nan Ron, by which Kyle of Tongue may be most conveniently approached from the east.

Tides

The west-going stream begins about +0350 Ullapool (−0030 Dover).
The east-going stream begins about −0220 Ullapool (+0545 Dover).
The spring rate is about 2 knots.

Eilean nan Ron

Mol na Coinnle 58°33'N 04°20'W is distinguished from Port na h'Uaille a cable further N by ruins and a roofed building on the skyline.

Drying reefs extend from either shore at the entrance; approach in mid-channel, only in westerly winds, and only if there is no swell.

Mol na Coinnle, Eilean nan Ron; only to be visited in very quiet conditions

119

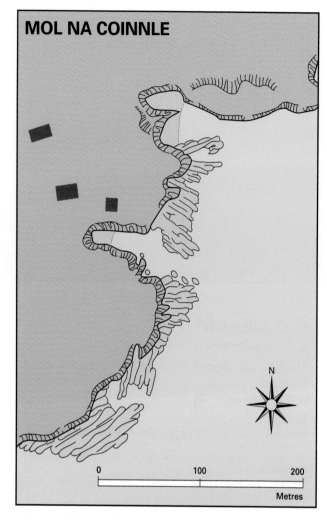

MOL NA COINNLE

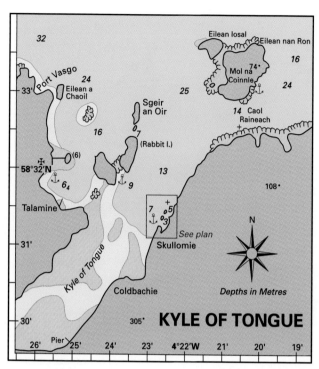

KYLE OF TONGUE

Depths in Metres

A concrete quay on the north side has water at all states of tide and mooring rings, but rocks below water project beyond the face of the quay so that it is unsafe for a yacht to remain alongside.

Kyle of Tongue

58°33'N 04°24'W

Chart

OS Explorer *447*

Tides

The in-going stream begins about –0505 Ullapool (+0300 Dover).

The outgoing stream begins about +0110 Ullapool (–0310 Dover).

Constant –0000 Ullapool (+0338 Dover)

Dangers and marks

The inner part of the kyle is beset by sandbanks and shoals.

Dubh-sgeir Mhor lies 4 cables southeast of Eilean a' Chaoil at the northwest point of the Kyle, with a drying rock SW of it.

See also Talmine, below.

In the channel between Rabbit Islands and Sgeir an Oir a submerged rock north of mid-channel could be a hazard to a keel boat at low water.

Approach

From east through Caol Raineach (for tides see above).

From west pass north and east of Sgeir an Oir which lies north of Rabbit Is (see also Talmine, below). There are no navigational lights in the Kyle.

Skullomie

58°31'N 04°23'W

This inlet on the E side of the entrance to the Kyle has a stone quay on its west side, the projecting head of which has collapsed, and stones on the bottom may obstruct the berths alongside the face of the main quay.

Apart from the remains of the old pier head there is a depth of at least 1·2m within the harbour.

Two skerries above water lie north of the quay (which is not visible from seaward); the more southerly of these must be passed on its north side, owing to submerged rocks to the south of it.

Supplies

May be found at Tongue, about 4M distant, or at Talmine.

Rabbit Islands

58°32'N 04°24'W

Rabbit Islands provide some shelter from north and west in the bight to the SE of the tidal gap between the two largest islands. A submerged rock lies half a cable off the south point of the bay.

Skullomie

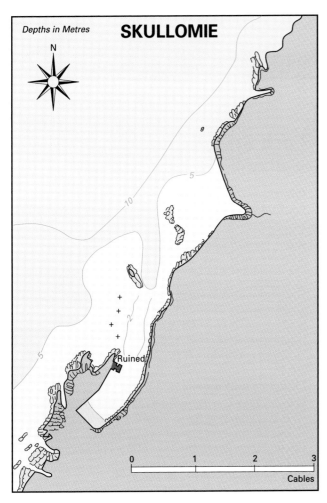

Rabbit Islands

Talmine

58°32'N 04°26'W

Eilean Creagach is joined to the northwest shore by a stone pier, which provides shelter for several local boats.

Rabbit Islands, joined to the mainland by a drying sand bar and boulders, provide some shelter from the east, forming a bay open only to north.

Talmine Bay

Dubh-sgeir Bheag lies about 2 cables NE of Eilean Creagach.

Approach

From west pass north of Eilean a'Chaoil, and head for the north end of Sgeir an Oir until the west point of Rabbit Island touches Ard Skinid at the west side of Kyle of Tongue to pass east of Dubh-sgeir Mhor. Hold close to Rabbit Island until past its west point, to avoid Dubh-sgeir Bheag.

A yacht can go alongside the southwest side of the pier at high water, and can dry out alongside.

Supplies

Shop, PO, telephone, hotel.

Loch Eriboll

⊕ 3M NNW of Whiten Head 58°37'N 04°38'W

Charts

BA *2076* (1:17,500); OS Landranger *9*; OS Explorer *447*

Tides

Within the loch tidal streams are insignificant, but off Whiten Head they run up to 3 knots.

The in-going stream begins about −0505 Ullapool (+0300 Dover).

The outgoing stream begins about +0110 Ullapool (−0310 Dover).

Constant −0000 Aberdeen (+0338 Dover)

Heights in metres

MHWS	MHWN	MTL	MLWN	MLWS
4·2	4·0	3·1	2·2	0·9

Dangers and marks

Whiten Head, with prominent white stacks, Stacan Bana, standing up to 2 cables NW and west of it, lies on the east side of the entrance.

Eilean Hoan lies to the west of the entrance, with An Dubh-sgeir, an islet 10m high, ENE of it and submerged rocks between them.

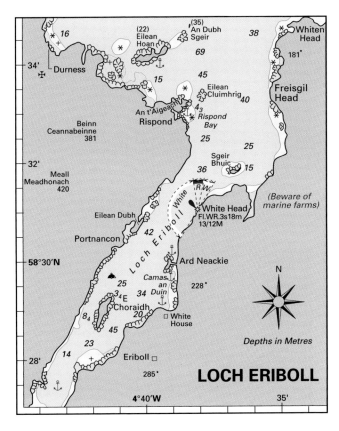

LOCH ERIBOLL

Eilean Cluimhrig (Klourig), a mile SE of Eilean Hoan, has a drying rocky shore, and Sparrow Rock, which just dries, lies 2 cables west of its north end.

Approach

From west, although there are deep passages west of Eilean Hoan and between that island and An Dubh-sgeir, it would be unwise for a stranger to attempt them without the large-scale chart.

Light

White head (not Whiten head, which is 4M NNE) Fl.WR.3s18m13/12M. Shows red 172°-191° and white elsewhere

Eilean Hoan provides some shelter from NW on its SE side in 10-15m, but is prone to swell.

Rispond Bay

58°37'N 04°48'W

A small inlet a mile SW of Eilean Cluimhrig. The passage between Eilean Cluimhrig and Sparrow Rock can be taken in quiet weather, with care, if the position of the latter is clearly established.

If passing east of Eilean Cluimhrig, note that the reefs off its shore extend about a cable SE and south of the island.

Rispond Rock, which dries 0·9m, lies 1 cable east of the south point of the entrance to Rispond Bay.

Rispond

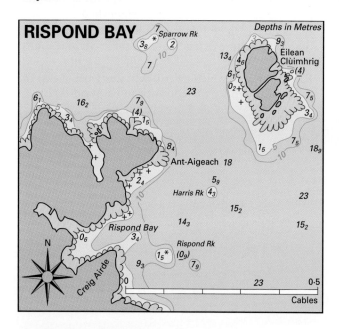

RISPOND BAY

Depths in Metres

Sparrow Rk

Eilean Clùimhrig

Ant-Aigeach 18

Harris Rk

Rispond Bay

Rispond Rk

Creig Airde

Cables

Ard Neackie

A fish farm may occupy the head of the bay, but there is anchoring depth east of it. A drying harbour in an inlet on the NW side of the bay can be entered at half tide. Stores at Durness, at least 4M by road.

Ard Neackie
A promontory on the east side of loch, south of White Head, with bays to N and S, providing shelter according to wind direction. The north bay has patches of weed.

Camas an Duin
Most of this bay is occupied by a fish farm.

Portnancon
On the west shore of the loch off an old stone pier immediately opposite Ard Neackie. It is reported that the pier is the property of the ferry house and visiting boats are not welcome to use it.

Head of loch has moderate depths, mud, but is subject to squalls in SW winds.

Other inlets providing a degree of shelter and suitable anchoring depths may be found with the large-scale chart in quiet conditions.

Geodha Smoo
Visited in about 1910 by *Blue Dragon II*, which, characteristically, found a rock which did not appear on the chart at the time. No other visits are known.

Durness
A temporary anchorage in Saligo Bay, 58°34'N 04°44'W, to go ashore for stores.

Supplies
Petrol and diesel, *Calor Gas*, PO, telephone, hotel.

Kyle of Durness
⊕ 1M NW of Faraid Head 58°37'N 04°48'W

Exposed to the northwest, but in suitable conditions might provide a convenient temporary anchorage off the sandy beach in Balnakeil Bay, in the southeast corner.

Stores at Durness, more than a mile east of Balnakeil.

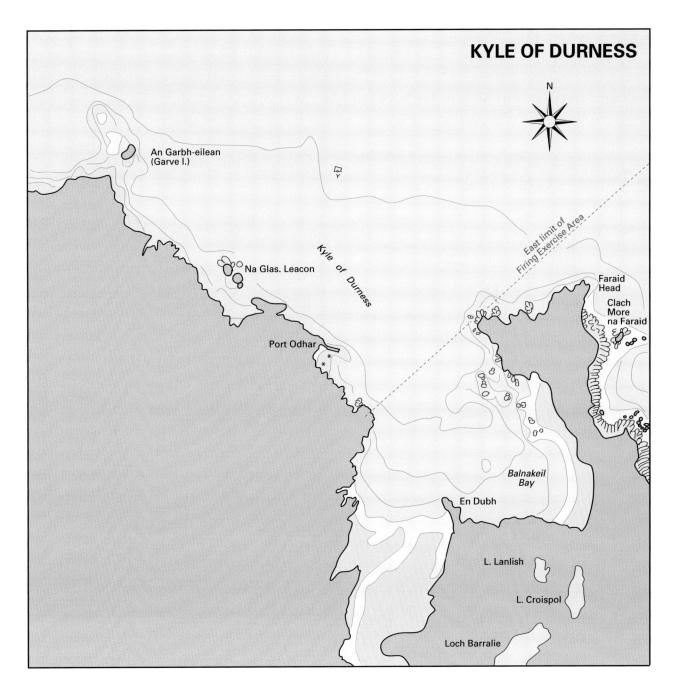

KYLE OF DURNESS

An Garbh-eilean
(Garve I.)

Na Glas. Leacon

Kyle of Durness

East limit of
Firing Exercise Area

Faraid
Head

Clach
More
na Faraid

Port Odhar

Balnakeil
Bay

En Dubh

L. Lanlish

L. Croispol

Loch Barralie

Faraid Head to Cape Wrath and West Coast

Tides

Between Faraid Head and Stac Clo Kearvaig, the headland 2M east of Cape Wrath

The west-going stream begins about +0350 Ullapool (–0030 Dover).

The east-going stream begins about –0220 Ullapool (+0545 Dover).

Between Stac Clo Kearvaig and Cape Wrath

The west-going stream begins about +0235 Ullapool (–0145 Dover).

The east-going stream begins about –0350 Ullapool (+0415 Dover).

Off Cape Wrath an eddy causes an almost continuous west-going stream close inshore, and southwest of Cape Wrath there is an almost continuous north-going stream, with turbulence where these streams meet.

A bombing range extends several miles from the shore in an arc from a point 2M northeast of Faraid Head to a point a mile east of Cape Wrath.

When this range is in use a guard boat on station nearby can be called on VHF Ch 16. Prospective use of the range is included in Maritime Safety Information broadcasts on VHF. Kyle of Durness is outside the range itself.

Distances

Eilean Hoan lies 11M E of Cape Wrath. Kinlochbervie is 16M SSW, and Stornoway is 50M SW of Cape Wrath.

Dangers and marks

Faraid Head 7M east of Cape Wrath is a headland 98m high with a prominent building ¼M south of its tip.

An Garbh-eilean, 3 cables offshore 3M WNW of Faraid Head, is 31m high.

A yellow target buoy lies 1½M northwest of Faraid Head

Cape Wrath is 110m high, with a white lighthouse near its edge.

Duslic Rock, 7 cables northeast of Cape Wrath lighthouse, dries 3·4m.

Am Balg 6 M SSW of Cape Wrath is a detached rock 44m high.

To pass north of Duslic Rock keep the summit of Faraid Head open north of An Garbh-eilean bearing 109°.

To pass NW of Duslic Rock keep Am Balg just open NW of Cape Wrath bearing 215°.

To pass south of Duslic Rock keep the south edge of An Garbh-eilean in line with the north edge of Faraid Head bearing 102°. The sea in this passage is usually disturbed and sometimes dangerous.

Light

Cape Wrath LtHo Fl(4)30s122m22M

Cape Wrath from west

Appendix

I. OTHER PILOTS AND PILOTS TO ADJACENT AREAS

North Coast of Scotland Pilot, Third edition (1994), NP52 (Hydrographic Office), includes Orkney and Shetland, and Faeroe Islands.

North Sea (West) Pilot, Third edition (1995), NP54 (Hydrographic Office).

(Note: Admiralty Pilots are replaced by new editions every three years or so; there are no Annual Supplements, but any significant amendments appear in *Notices to Mariners*.)

Sailing Directions of the Royal Northumberland Yacht Club, Humber to Rattray Head (2002)

Sailing Directions and Anchorages, North and North East Coasts of Scotland, 1976, (Clyde Cruising Club).

Forth, Tyne, Dogger, Humber Blakeney to St Abbs, Henry Irving (Imray, 2002)

Adjacent areas:

North Sea Passage Pilot, Brian Navin (Imray, 2003)

Faroe, Iceland and Greenland, RCC Pilotage Foundation (Imray 1998)

The Yachtsman's Pilot– Skye and the Northwest Coast of Scotland, Martin Lawrence (Imray, 2002)

The Yachtsman's Pilot Clyde to Colonsay, Martin Lawrence (Imray, 2001)

The Yachtsman's Pilot to the Isle of Mull and adjacent waters, Martin Lawrence (Imray 2003)

Fishermen's Pilots NP150 and 151 (UKHO)

Forth Yacht Clubs Association *Pilot Handbook* from Bosun's Locker, Port Edgar and other chandlers.

Directory of Northeast Council Harbours (includes tide tables), published annually free of charge. Aberdeenshire Council, Carlton House, Arduthie Road, Stonehaven AB39 2DP

OS *Explorer maps* at 1:25,000 are occasionally useful where there is no Admiralty chart at a sufficiently large scale. These have replaced the green covered *Pathfinder* series, and the series should be complete by the time this volume is published. An index sheet of all OS maps is available from Ordnance Survey, Romsey Road, Southampton SO1 4GU ☎ 08456 050505 *Fax* 023 8079 2615 and from larger bookshops, as well as on the internet at www.ordnancesurvey.co.uk

Some charts which have been discontinued provide much more detail, at a large scale, than any now published for the same area. All older charts, particularly the fine Victorian engravings, show more detail inshore and on land than the current publications, although they may be less accurate. Old charts should only be used to supplement current ones, not as a substitute for them.

The following old charts in particular may be found useful:

2170 Dornoch Firth and Approaches (1:25,000)

1783 Thurso Bay (1:14,280)

Photocopies of old charts – of editions not less than 50 years old, for copyright reasons – may be obtained from the National Library of Scotland Map Room Annexe, 33 Salisbury Place, Edinburgh 9 ☎ 031 226 4531

II. CHARTS

Admiralty pilots and OS Landranger

Chart no	Title	Scale
Chapter I		
111	Berwick to Farne Islands	1:35,000
129	Whitby to Flamborough Head	1:75,000
152	River Tyne to River Tees	1:75,000
156	Farne Islands to River Tyne	1:75,000
160	St Abb's Head to Farne Islands	1:75,000
1612	Plans: Scarborough, Whitby, Runswick Bay, North Sunderland, Holy Island, Berwick, Eyemouth	(various)
1627	Plans: Sunderland, Seaham, Warkworth	(various)
Landranger		
OS 81	Alnwick and Morpeth	1:50,000
OS 75	Berwick on Tweed	1:50,000
OS 67	Duns, Dunbar and Eyemouth	1:50,000
Chapters II and III		
1407	Montrose to Berwick	1:200,000
175	Fife Ness to St Abb's Head	1:75,000
733	Firth of Forth – Burntisland to Dalgety Bay	1:7,500
734	Firth of Forth – Isle of May to Inchkeith	1:50,000
735	Firth of Forth – Approaches to Leith and Burntisland	
	Leith	1:10,000
	Approaches to Leith and Burntislands	1:25,000
736	Firth of Forth – Granton and Burntisland to Rosyth	1:15,000
737	River Forth – Rosyth to Kincardine	1:17,500
	Crombie Jetty	1:7,500
741	Plans in the Firth of Forth and River Forth	
	Alloa to Stirling	1:20,000
	Kincardine to Alloa	1:20,000
	Grangemouth and River Carron	1:10,000
	Methil	1:10,000
Landranger		
OS 66	Edinburgh	1:50,000
OS 59	St Andrews	1:50,000
Chapter IV		
733	Burntisland to Dalgety Bay	1:7,500
736	Granton and Burntisland to Rosyth	1:15,000
737	Rosyth to Grangemouth	1:15,000
741	Plans in the Firth of Forth and River Forth	
	Alloa to Stirling	1:20,000
	Kincardine to Alloa	1:20,000
	Grangemouth and River Carron	1:10,000
	Methil	1:10,000
Landranger		
OS 65	Falkirk and West Lothian	1:50,000

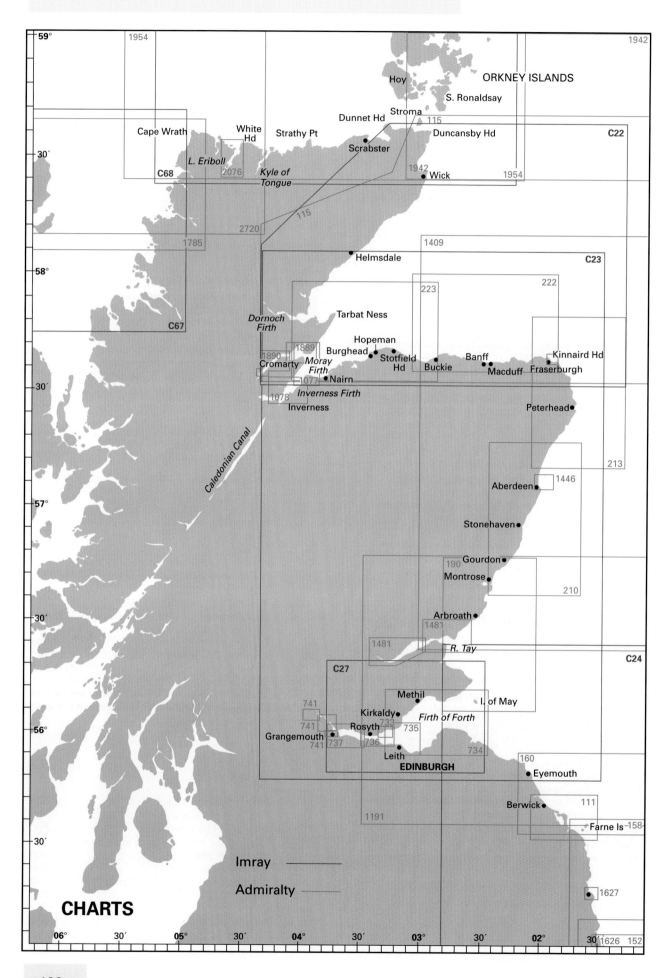

CHARTS

Imray ——————

Admiralty ———————

Chart no	Title	Scale

Chapter V
1407	Montrose to Berwick	1:200,000
1409	Buckie to Arbroath	1:200,000
190	Montrose to Fife Ness	1:75,000
210	Newburgh to Montrose	1:75,000
213	Fraserburgh to Newburgh	1:75,000
1481	River Tay	1:75,000
1438	Plans of Arbroath, Montrose, Stonehaven, Peterhead	(various)
1446	Aberdeen	1:15,000

Landranger
OS 59	St Andrews	1:50,000
OS 54	Dundee to Montrose	1:50,000
OS 45	Stonehaven	1:50,000
OS 38	Aberdeen	1:50,000
OS 30	Fraserburgh and Peterhead	1:50,000

Chapter VI
115	Moray Firth	1:200,000
222	Buckie to Fraserburgh	1:75,000
223	Dunrobin Point to Buckie	1:75,000
1462	Plans of Fraserburgh, Macduff and Banff, Buckie, Lossiemouth	(various)

Landranger
OS 30	Fraserburgh	1:50,000
OS 29	Banff	1:50,000
OS 28	Elgin and Dufftown	1:50,000

Chapter VII
223	Dunrobin Point to Buckie	1:75,000
1889	Cromarty Firth	1:15,000
1890	Cromarty Firth (Inner part)	1:15,000
1077	Approaches to Inverness Firth	1:20,000
1078	Inverness Firth	1:20,000
1791	Caledonian Canal	1:75,000
1462	Plans of Hopeman, Burghead, Nairn	(various)

Landranger
OS 27	Nairn	1:50,000
OS 26	Inverness	1:50,000
OS 21	Dornoch, Alness, Invergordon	1:50,000

Chapter VIII
115	Moray Firth	1:200,000
223	Dunrobin Point to Buckie	1:75,000
1462	Plans of Helmsdale, Wick	(various)

Landranger
OS 21	Dornoch, Alness, Invergordon	1:50,000
OS 17	Helmsdale	1:50,000
OS 11	Thurso and Dunbeath	1:50,000

Chapter IX
1954	Cape Wrath to Pentland Firth	1:200,000
2162	Pentland Firth	1:50,000
2581	S Approaches to Scapa Flow	1:26,000
1462	includes plans of Scrabster (various)	

Landranger
OS 12	Thurso and Wick	1:50,000
OS 10	Strathnaver	1:50,000
OS 9	Cape Wrath	1:50,000

Imray
C70	Southern North Sea passage chart	1:950,000
C29	Harwich to Whitby	1:250,000
	Plans River Humber, Hull Marina, Filey, Bridlington, Scarborough, Whitby	
C25	*Plans* IJmuiden, Scheveneningen, Den Helder, Oudeschild	1:340,000
C24	Flamborough Head to Fife Ness	1:251,700
	Plans Whitby, River Tees, Hartlepool, Seaham,	

Chart no	Title	Scale

	Sunderland, River Tyne, Blyth, Warkworth, Holy Island Harbour, Berwick, Eyemouth	
C27	Firth of Forth	1:77,000
	Plans Dunbar, North Berwick, Port Seton, Cockenzie, Leith, Inchkeith, Granton, Crail, Anstruther, St Monance, Pittenweem, Methil, Dysart, Kirkcaldy, Burntisland, Dalgety Bay, North Queeensferry, Port Edgar, Limekilns and Brucehaven, Grangemouth, St Andrews	
C23	Firth of Forth to Moray Firth	1:250,000
	Plans Helmsdale, Inverness Firth, Inverness, Burghead, Hopeman, Buckie, Banff & Macduff, Fraserburgh, Peterhead, Aberdeen, Stonehaven, Montrose, Arbroath	
C22	Moray Firth	1:165,000
	Plans Fraserburgh, Banff and Macduff, Buckie, Lossiemouth, Burghead, Hopeman, Helmsdale	
C68	Cape Wrath to Wick and Orkney Islands	1:162,100
	Plans Wick, Scrabster, Kirkwall, Stromness, Pierowall, Whitewall	

Admiralty chart agents within the area covered by this volume

Newcastle Lilley & Gillie Ltd, North Shields
☎ 0191 257 2217
Edinburgh Chattan Security Ltd, Easter Road
☎ 0131 5547527
Dundee Sea & Shore Marine Supplies, Victoria Dock
☎ 01382 202666
Aberdeen Thomas Gunn Ltd, Regent Quay
☎ 01224 595 045
Findhorn The Boatyard ☎ 01309 690099
Inverness Caley Marina, Canal Road
☎ 01463 236539.

Imray Laurie Norie & Wilson Ltd are Admiralty chart agents and will supply charts by post; Wych House, The Broadway, St Ives, Cambridgeshire PE27 5BT
☎ 01480 462114 *Fax* 01480 496109
Imrays are also agents for Ordnance Survey.

III. TIDAL STREAMS

On the following pages tidal streams for the north and east costs of Scotland and the Pentland Firth are related to high water Dover.
The figures show rates at spring and neap tides e.g. *04,09* means the rate is 0.4 knots at neaps and 0.9 knots at springs.

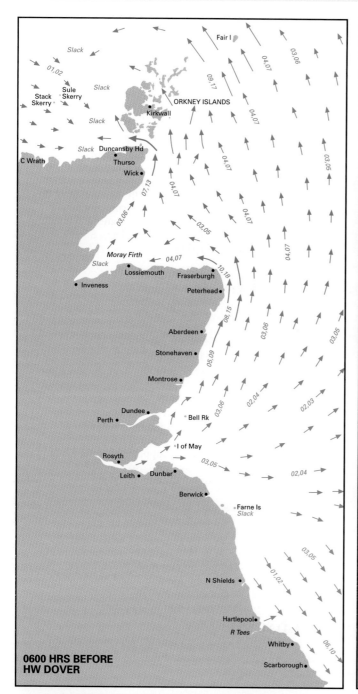

0600 HRS BEFORE HW DOVER

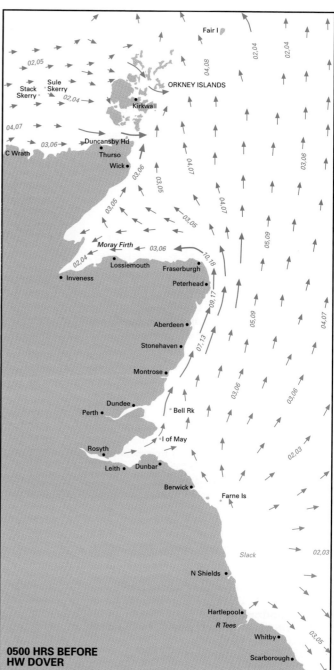

0500 HRS BEFORE HW DOVER

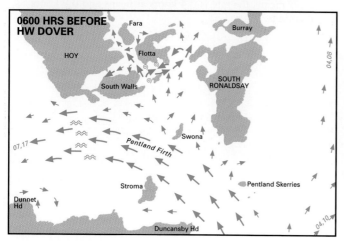

0600 HRS BEFORE HW DOVER

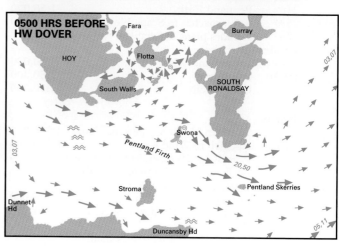

0500 HRS BEFORE HW DOVER

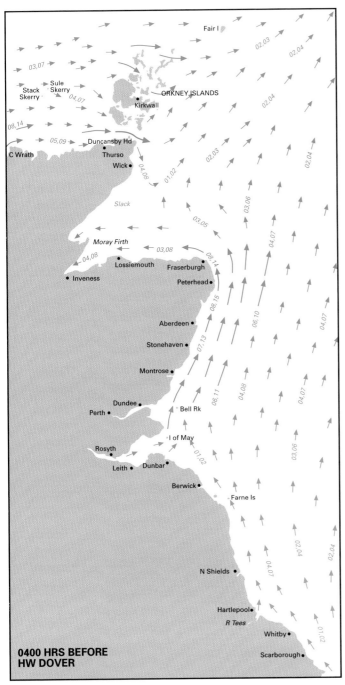

0400 HRS BEFORE
HW DOVER

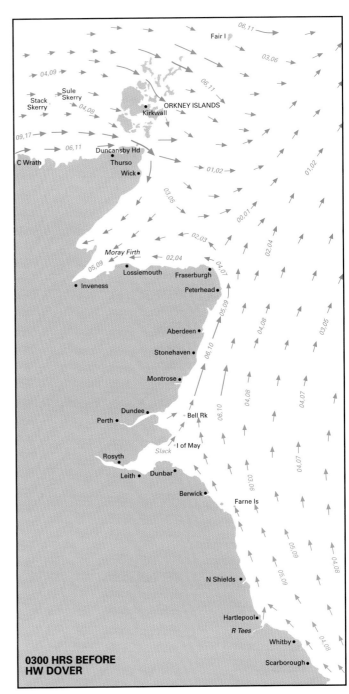

0300 HRS BEFORE
HW DOVER

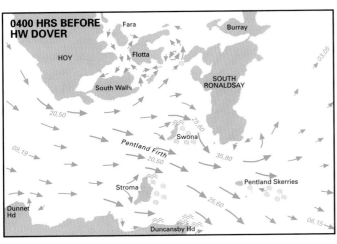

0400 HRS BEFORE
HW DOVER

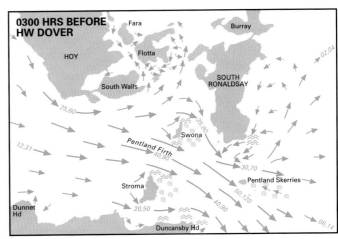

0300 HRS BEFORE
HW DOVER

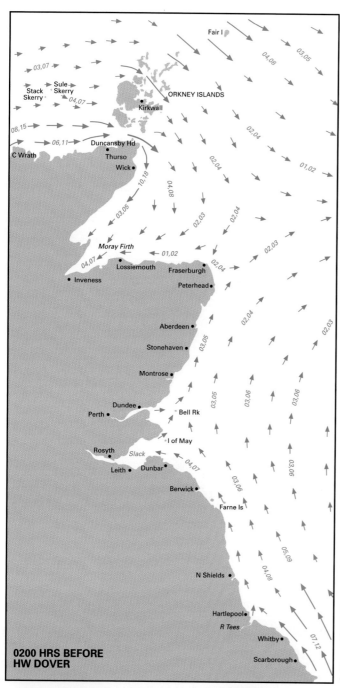

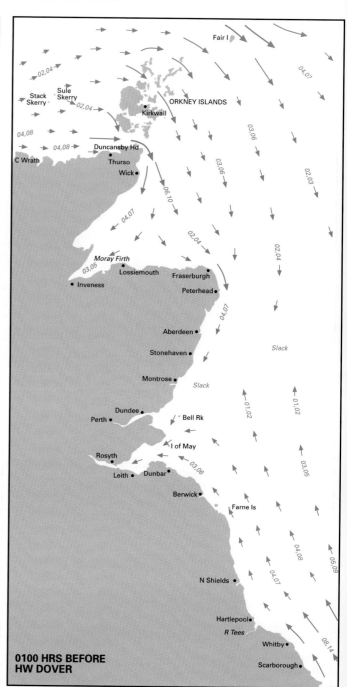

0200 HRS BEFORE HW DOVER

0100 HRS BEFORE HW DOVER

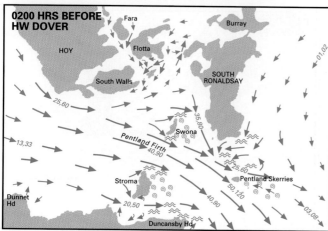

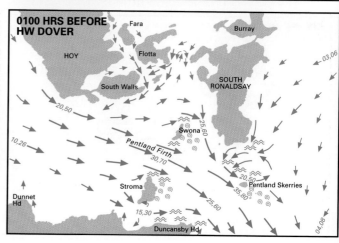

0200 HRS BEFORE HW DOVER

0100 HRS BEFORE HW DOVER

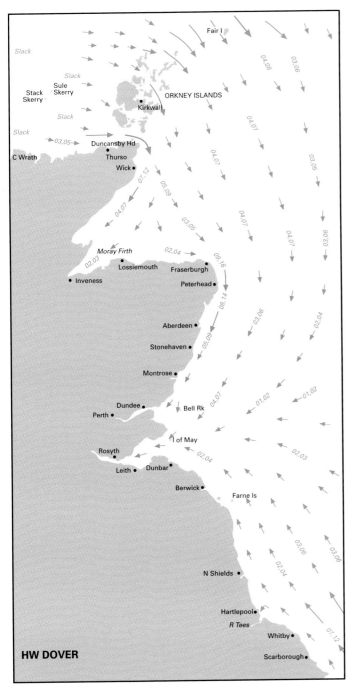

HW DOVER

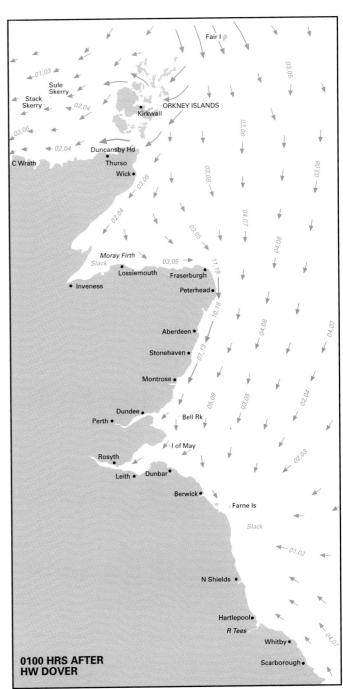

0100 HRS AFTER
HW DOVER

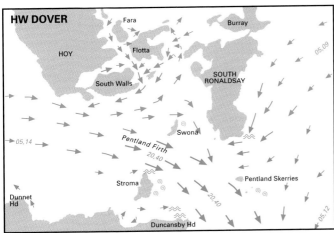

HW DOVER

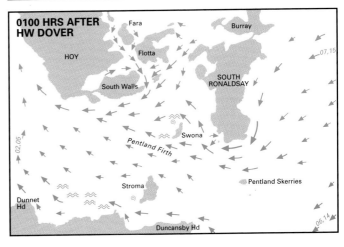

0100 HRS AFTER
HW DOVER

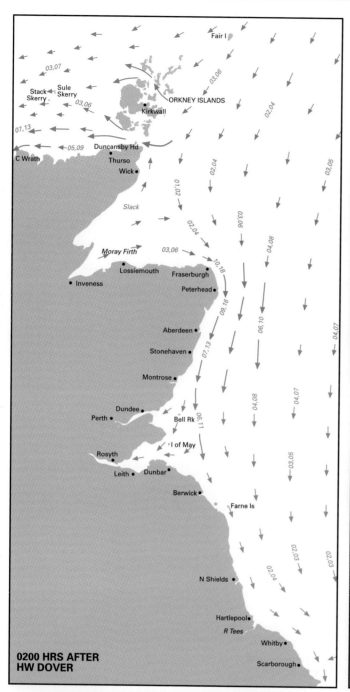

0200 HRS AFTER HW DOVER

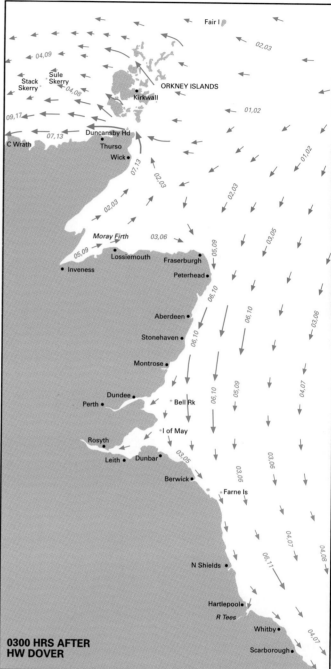

0300 HRS AFTER HW DOVER

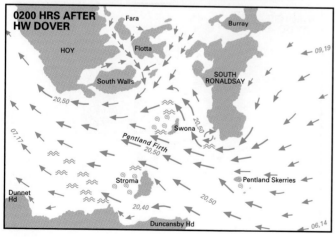

0200 HRS AFTER HW DOVER

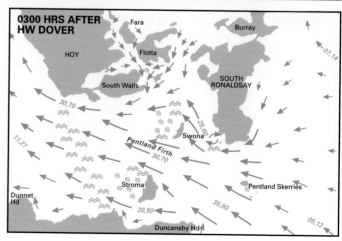

0300 HRS AFTER HW DOVER

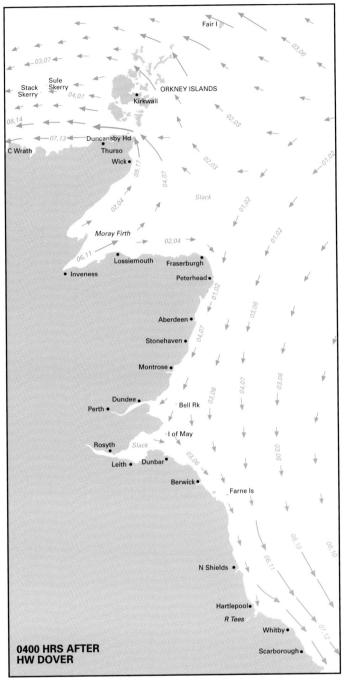

0400 HRS AFTER HW DOVER

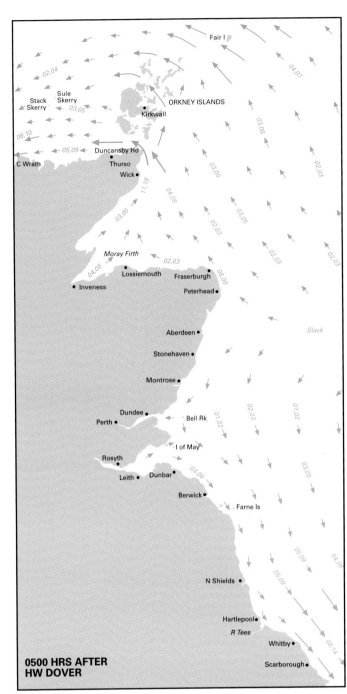

0500 HRS AFTER HW DOVER

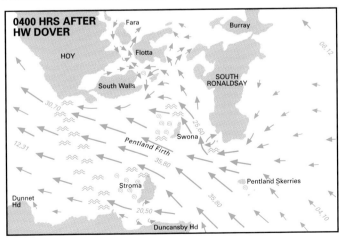

0400 HRS AFTER HW DOVER

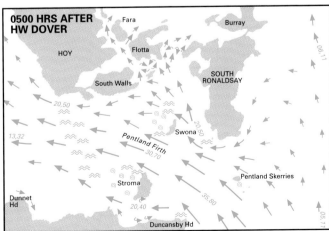

0500 HRS AFTER HW DOVER

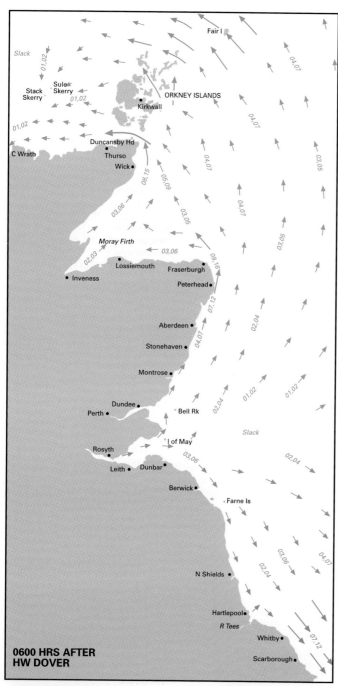

0600 HRS AFTER HW DOVER

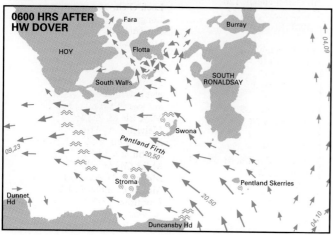

0600 HRS AFTER HW DOVER

Index